A SAMPLING OF DUTCH LITERATURE

GARMT STUIVELING

A sampling of Dutch literature

*Thirteen excursions into the works of
Dutch authors*

Translated and adapted by James Brockway

Published by
RADIO NEDERLAND WERELDOMROEP
HILVERSUM THE NETHERLANDS

The pattern followed in this series of thirteen broadcasts may seem an unusual one—that is to say, twelve sources of inspiration were chosen as themes for introducing samples of Dutch and Flemish literature from its beginnings to the present day.

Even if unusual, this appeared to be an appropriate framework for a weekly radio series spread over three months and designed to appeal to audiences overseas.

The publishers

CONTENTS

	page
Note by the translator	7
Introduction	9
Spring	14
Love	20
Laughter	25
Religion	31
Death	37
The Motherland	43
Amsterdam	49
Rembrandt	55
The Sea	61
The Farmer	67
Freedom	74
The Child	80
Supplement: Youth	87
Index	99

Tape recordings of the series are available free of charge on application to the Transcription Service of Radio Nederland, Hilversum, The Netherlands.

Een nieu Geu=
sen Lieden Boecxken /

Waerinne begrepen is / den gantschen
Handel der Nederlantscher ghesciede-
nissen / dees voorleden Jaeren tot noch
toe ghedragen / eensdeels onderwy-
len in Druck wtghegaen / eensdeels nu nieu vp-ghe-
uoecht.

Nu nieulick vermeerdert ende verbetert.

Viue Dieu, La Santé du Roy, & la Pros-
perité des Geus. Anno 1581.

Title-page of "Geuzenliedboek" (epic songs from the "Water-Beggars" fight for independence) containing the "Wilhelmus" text (1581 edition)

NOTE BY THE TRANSLATOR

These 'excursions' were translated and adapted for Radio Nederland from an original set written in Dutch by Professor Garmt Stuiveling. They were designed as educational broadcasts and the aim was to present as many examples as possible of the Dutch and Flemish prose and poetry mentioned, in English translations. Since, especially where poetry is concerned, this involved the problem of whether the original work quoted lent itself to translation, I was allowed a free hand to adapt the Dutch versions when putting them into English. Apart from the last talk and some insertions here and there in the others (for which I must bear the responsibility), and apart also from a few adaptations made by Radio Nederland staff when producing the talks in the studio, the English versions nevertheless keep fairly closely to the pattern of the originals.

Professor Stuiveling had already used translations by Professor Barnouw and the one by Emile van Loo. As for the rest, in some cases I was able to use translations of poetry I had already made—of which some have appeared in print elsewhere—and in others there was nothing for it but to get down to translating poems which, though in my opinion they did not always lend themselves very well to translation, had to be included, since in a survey of this kind their authors should be represented. A translation cannot but be a more or less distorted reflection of the original work, and in the case of a poem the distortion will usually be rather more than less. However, perhaps enough of the originals has been reflected to suggest their nature and special qualities in Dutch. It is my hope that the poets concerned, if still living, will not frown too severely on the result, and, if dead, will not turn over in their graves. J. B.

INTRODUCTION *

Holland is a comparatively small country. It has at present very nearly twelve million inhabitants, and if the five million Dutch-speaking Flemings, residing in Belgium, are added, it still only adds up to seventeen million. This total is naturally in great excess of the population who inhabited the same area a century ago, not mentioning the population of three, four or eight centuries ago. However, the total population is of lesser importance than the intrinsic cultural potential. How many inhabitants were in classical Athens or Florence in the Dantean period? Even minute Holland has added, in great measure, to the culture of humanity.

When one confines oneself to art, one name alone reflects the debt the world owes Holland in this sphere - Rembrandt. Through him we are on a par with genius, as England was with Shakespeare, Germany with Bach and Beethoven and Austria with Mozart. It seems each nation reaches its zenith in a specific field, because Holland also produced Vincent van Gogh (not inferior in fame to Rembrandt) who revolutionised painting and was, in fact, the instigator or father of modern art. Through him the world must again be thankful to Holland.

Dutch literature has unfortunately not reached such heights of genius as in the case of Rembrandt and Van Gogh. That is to say, not in Dutch itself. But it is well to recall two masterpieces in world literature by two Dutch authors, although written in the language of the period, namely, latin. The one work, "De Imitatione Christi", embracing the imitation of Christ, was written in the fifteenth century most probably by Thomas van Kempen (Thomas à Kempis) and is at present distributed throughout the world in numerous editions and various translations. In his blending of reflective and practical directed piety, a typical Dutch characteristic is exposed. Although the religious convictions have deviated or altered in the past five centuries, the Dutch mentality is even now clearly recognisable in the text.

The second book, not less renowned, is "The Praise of Folly" written by the great humanist Erasmus. Only half a century separated the

* Translated by Radio Nederland.

"Imitatio" and the last named work, yet, the contrast is enormous. As a result of his journeys through West and South Europe, Erasmus obtained first hand knowledge of the entire civilised world of that century pertaining to the reigning Christianity. He mixed with people from different walks of life as well as character; he met monarchs and cardinals. The abuses of responsibility around the year 1500 aroused his indignation. He stated that the entire mankind, whether from high or low birth, was ruled by evil desires; a toy of every iniquitous urge. It was a stroke of genius by Erasmus to have the personification of Folly deliver her own panegyric, thus allowing himself to direct razor-sharp criticism without being immediately reproached. Right up to the present time "The Praise of Folly" is one of the most masterly satires in world literature, although it is read by each nation in the translatory form rather than in the original latin.

Thomas van Kempen and Erasmus make us rather regret the fact that Holland did not retain latin as its written language. For those, however, who speak and read Dutch, it is manifest that Dutch literature is also of great significance, although up till now there have been few endeavours to popularise it by means of translations. Literature, however, is so directly related to language, especially in poetry where such extensive use is made of the language peculiarities, that translations inevitably lessen the artistic value and in a few specific cases even necessitate intrinsic changes. Unlike music or art, language is not innately international. But it is independent of national borders, allowing two or more countries the same language, or in reverse, more than one language to one country. The present Netherlands State came into being as an independent State in and by the uprising, led by William the Silent, against Spain. Thus the Netherlands State is barely four centuries old. The literature, however, written in the regions which at present belong to Holland and Flemish Belgium, goes back much further. The remaining manuscripts from the middle ages date back to the 12th century. They were written in dialects, which later formed the basis of modern Dutch. One may, therefore, assume Dutch literature to have existed for eight centuries.

Originally the Southern Netherlands was the area of the greatest economic prosperity and, therefore, also had the greatest spiritual

10

maturity which was enhanced by the proximity of the French cultural area. Important contributions were also made by the Western regions with cities such as Bruges, Ghent and later Antwerp; and also the Eastern part, that is, in the vicinity of the Limburgian town of Maastricht. In between the tales of chivalry, mostly relating to the emperor Charlemagne, there were a few noteworthy works of regional literature, though most were translations from the original French texts. Also in the lives of the Saints in rhyme, or legends pertaining to the Virgin Mary, there is something quite exceptional. The most important of these is the moving history of Beatrix, a nun, who because of her earthly love, left her convent, lived for seven years with her lover in a distant land and there gave birth to two children. Her lover then left her whereupon the spent seven sinful years in order to obtain food for her children and then returned to the convent in great repentance. There she discovered the Mary image had carried out her tasks for her over the fourteen years so that her sinful disappearance went unnoticed.

Pride of place in the Dutch middle ages belongs to the theatrical plays, which were partially secular and partially spiritual. It is quite remarkable that the Southern Netherlands possess three romantic plays from the second half of the fourteenth century which are older than any similar play in the whole of Western Europe. From a cultural-historical point it is of the utmost importance, as for example the origin of the West European theatre, by this fact, would have been interpreted differently than is generally the case. Out of the series of spiritual plays from the Southern Netherlands, the "Elckerlyc" became world famous due to its translation into "The Everyman". The question, whether the Dutch or the English play should be considered as the original, has, upon style analysis, been credited to the Dutch.

Two other facts must still be mentioned in connection with the literary growth in the middle ages. Firstly, that the international theme of Reinaert de Vos, in Flanders, was revised and became a masterpiece of its type; a long narrative poem, whose form is a parody of the tales of chivalry while the contents satirize the whole system of mediaeval feudalism in the state and church. The other fact is, that in the Netherlands the song or Lied came into its own and many beautiful lyrical poems were composed as a result of this; some ballads, some love songs and others spiritual songs. Undoubtedly they were often sung but even without the melody, they possessed an unusual quality.

After a period of recession, the influence of the Renaissance made itself felt in the Netherlands in the middle of the 16th century. It was a period of tremendous tension in religious as well as political fields which had reverberations in literature. The Dutch national anthem, The Wilhelmus, was composed in this period. It is of importance that during this period the focus of economic prosperity was transferred from the South, from Antwerp, to the North, to Amsterdam. This was accelerated by the successful uprising against Spain by the Northern Provinces, while the Southern Provinces were still occupied. From 1600 till 1700, Amsterdam was one of the most important cultural centres in Europe where arts and science, as well as trade and politics developed apace. The three greatest poets of the time were Amsterdammers; Joost van den Vondel, Pieter Corneliszoon Hooft and Gerbrandt Adriaenszoon Bredero. Their work is versatile and the style is elegant; it has the eminent greatness of the classics, not only in drama but also in comedy. The dramas of Vondel (1587-1679) reached their dramatic zenith in "Lucifer" (1654), a religious tragedy with no lesser value than "Paradise Lost", which deals with the same subject. Hooft (1581-1647) is the finest lyrical poet in Dutch literature, but at the same time the author of a tremendous work embracing the history of the rising against Spain; a work which may be classed in the top ten historical works in the world. Bredero (1585-1618) gave us songs and comedies which reflected life in Amsterdam as did the paintings of Jan Steen or Frans Hals.

Besides Vondel, Hooft and Bredero there were scores of lesser poets with noticeable talent. Of them, Constantijn Huygens (1596-1679) deserves special mention for his literary contacts with England and especially John Donne.

In the eighteenth century the renovation commenced as around 1780 the Romantics were produced. It was then that prose, for the first time, got the upper hand as an art form. The novel in letters, "Sara Burgerhart" by the ladies Wolff and Deken belongs to the first crop. In 1839 there appeared the popular book, with typical Dutch novels, "Camera Obscura" by the parson, Beets, and in 1860 a Dutch East Indian civil servant, with the nom-de-plume Multatuli, surprised the Dutch nation with a stirring masterpiece entitled "Max Havelaar" which has been distributed in numerous editions and numerous languages and is acknowledged as a Dutch contribution to world literature. It is only comparable to "Uncle Tom's Cabin" but greater, more satirical, more profound.

Since 1880 Dutch literature has become wholly modern, branching out in many directions; France, England, Germany, a national expression of the modern trend discernible in the whole of Europe.

SPRING

In Holland the winters are long, and all through the ages Dutchmen have looked forward eagerly to the coming of Spring. In times gone by great bonfires would be lit at Eastertime to welcome Spring's approach, and in the merry month of May it was the custom for young suitors to make for their sweetheart's house, to offer her a branch of springtime blossom. The old ballads of the Middle Ages often sang of Spring, always entwining their theme with that other delightful subject, young love. Here are some verses from one such ballad:

THERE FELL A DEW FROM HEAVEN

There fell a dew from heaven
On my love's window sill
None lovelier saw I ever,
My heart is at her will.
My wounded heart is wholly
The captive of her spell,
If she would but console me,
Then all with me were well.

Winter has ceased his scolding
And May is holding Mass,
I see the leaves unfolding
And flowers sprout in the grass
It's good to go a-maying
In yonder shaded dale,
The songbirds there are vying
With master nightingale.

I'll go and render honor
To May at my love's door,
And be to her a donor
Of faith for ever more.
I'll sing: 'Do up thy bower,
Open the window wide!
Receive the May with flower
and leaf, and be my bride!'

Daer viel een hemels douwe
(Translated by Adriaan J. Barnouw)

14

When the Renaissance reached Holland's frontiers, there was a marked change in man's attitude to Nature. Renaissance culture was an urban, sophisticated culture, and the literary men in the towns had little contact with the countryside.

You will scarcely ever come across a poem inspired by flowers or animals or by a landscape in the countless lyrics of the 17th century. The Dutch poets left it to their painters to treat this subject, and these painters made the 17th century school of Dutch painting world-famous.

We owe one of the few 17th century poems which sings of the Spring to an Amsterdam poet, Jeremias de Decker, who lived from 1609 to 1666. In 13 four-line stanzas, he sings of all the joys of Spring, the sunny skies, the fresh, green fields and woods, the blossom and the birdsong, and of the inspiration all these give to the poet. It is a poem which relies greatly on sound for its charm, and so here are a few lines of it in the original Dutch, followed by a translation:

> Nu sich den Hemel open doet
> Met schooner lucht en sachter dagen,
> En 't aerdrijck voor soo felle vlagen
> Een minnend aensicht bied soo stoet...

in English:

> Now the Heavens open wide
> With purer skies and milder days,
> And earth to the fierce and gusty breeze
> Turns a face full gentle, like a bride.

Man's whole attitude to Nature changed again with the coming of the Romantic Movement in the late 18th century. Although many authors in Holland responded to this change before the 18th century was out, strangely enough, it was not until as late as the eighteen-eighties that its full effect was felt in Dutch poetry. Then the influence of early 19th century poets, such as Keats and Shelley, brought about a literary revolution in Holland and unleashed a flood of rich, lyrical poetry.

The men who brought about this revolution were known as the *Tachtigers*, the men of the 'eighties. One of them, Herman Gorter, wrote a great

15

lyrical poem entitled 'May'. This poem combines a then modern attitude towards Nature with a spontaneous, youthful philosophy of life and has become one of the great classics of Dutch literature. Here is a fragment in Adriaan J. Barnouw's translation:

'Twas dark indoors, but outside the still street
Gathered in dusk, and in the sky shone late
Daylight. A pale and golden glimmer fell
Across the gables on my window sill.
Then a boy blew, clear as an organ pipe,
The notes shook in the evening air, as ripe
As tender cherries when a breeze begins
Among the bush its airy wanderings.
He strolled across the bridges, and along
The water's edge, going slow, and scattering song
Like a young bird, and in unconsciousness
Of his own gladness with that evening peace.
And many a tired man, sitting at his ale
And supper, listened as to an ancient tale,
And smiled. A hand that pulled the window to
Paused for a moment as the piper blew.

That great Dutch novelist and prose stylist, Louis Couperus, who lived from 1863 to 1923, devoted one of his many elegant essays to his memories of Spring—in childhood, youth and later life. Here are some extracts from this essay:

I remember:

As a child, spring, Spring with a capital S, as something that existed in little poems in my schoolbooks...

I always imagined Spring as I had seen her once in a picture, as a gentle, beautiful, fair-haired young damsel, tripping over the daisies in her bare feet, and dressed in a gown, which I later discovered was called a 'peplos' in Greek. She held a set of antique pipes to her lips and smiled. But when I played in the dunes with my governess and, later, with my friends—it would be April or May—I never chanced across the young lady, and gradually I persuaded myself that the beautiful, young, fair-

Joost van den Vondel (1587-1679)

Constantijn Huygens (1596-1679)

Engraving from Vondel's drama "Lucifer" (1654). The chief rebel angel Lucifer is subjected by the archangel Michael. The loyal angels, drawn up in triangular formation, put down the rebel angels, whose battle array has the form of a half-moon.

haired damsel, with her pipes and her gown, was a Greek, and never set foot on the flowers which blossomed in our Dutch dunes...

I remember:

As a boy in the Indies, Spring, no, I don't remember any true Spring in the Indies...

There were dry and wet monsoons, and actually there were always those varnished green coconut palms and the flame trees with their scarlet blossoms; and the varnish was fresher or duller, depending on whether the sun scorched down or the rain streamed down. But Spring—a beautiful, fair-haired damsel, with a peplos and pipes—to tell you the truth, in Java I didn't give the child a second thought...

I remember:

Later, many years later, and it wasn't even in Greece, but only in the South of Italy...

A night... An automobile, which glided slowly and soundlessly down a long, white road through the white night. For the sky, the blue of a Spring night, had paled in an excess of moonlight that streamed and streamed... The automobile carried me on through the pale, blue Spring night, between endless orchards of almond blossom no eye could penetrate, and those trees blossomed in blossom of a thousand flowers, blossom on blossom, the petals sometimes drifting slowly across the roadway. It was so soft and white and ethereal—and yet of a tangible loveliness—that the automobile offended me, seeming crude and ugly, however noiselessly and however slowly it tried to roll along through this fairytale, this myth. And therefore the car came to a stop in the road, in the white road, in the white dust, in the white night, amid the white blossoms and the white rain of blossoms. And because everything was then quite quiet, and odorous with the balsam of the almond blossom, far in the distance, a nightingale began to sing his silver song... and then... then... suddenly... I understood that picture of long ago, that dear picture from my childhood, the gentle, beautiful, fair-haired young damsel... In the North, in those far-off days, she had been a fairy on a chocolate box, who didn't really exist, who had merely been drawn and painted, and had her praises sung by poets of varying talent in my school books. But here... here at last I heard in that silver song of the nightingale the trill of her pipes... Here she really *was*, here she really existed, here she had come to life...   (Translated by James Brockway)

17

The praises of Spring, of the month of May, have been sung again and again, hundreds of times over in poetry. So often, in fact, that the subject has become trite. Modern poets, however, have sometimes discovered a new and original approach to Couperus's fair-haired young damsel. Richard Minne, a Flemish poet, born in 1891, treated the theme in one of his poems with irony and humour, giving it an entirely new twist. Here is a translation of his poem.

BEAUTIFUL DAY

The budding tree, the bumble bee,
The wind which folly prompts and mirth,
In short, what men call Spring, that spree
That 'topsyturvifies' the earth,
Now froths and surges in my heart
I'd stick a flower in my hat,
If I were not a gentleman,
So proper, neat, unbent a man.

Did I but dare kick over the traces
I'd hug you all in huge embraces,
You, girls from the town, from the cattle stall,
You, man of learning, you, idle strutter,
You from the castle, you from the gutter,
Everything, tree and grass and all,
You, wandering butterfly, palely aflutter,
You, horse, you, sun, you, cloud, you, water,
And I'd dance with every maid and man,
If I were not a gentleman,
So proper, neat, unbent a man.

Dag van schoonheid
(Translated by James Brockway)

And here, to end with, is another poem with an original approach to Spring. During World War II, Holland was occupied for five years. To Dutchmen this period in their history was like a never-ending winter, and when at last liberation came, to them it was like the return of Spring. J. C. Bloem, born in 1887, one of the best-loved of contemporary Dutch poets, has written of this experience in two brief poems entitled, 'After the Liberation'. Here is a translation of the first of these poems. Bloem's poetry is celebrated for its intense yet muted emotion and its purity of form. The poem is unrhymed.

AFTER THE LIBERATION

Rare and radiant this Spring—as it was even then.
The mornings chill; but now, as the days unfold,
The eternal sky is a miracle to those
Who have come through.

A transparent haze hangs over the ravaged fields,
Where now, once more, slow horses tug the plough
As they did of old, while still the neighbouring air
Reverberates with war.

To have lived through this; to be able, unscathed, to say
These words; each morning, waking, to realize again:
It is past, it is done, for good, that slavery,
Scarcely to be endured.

It is rich and worth while, to have languished five long years,
Rebellious now and now again resigned:
No unborn child, not one, will ever know
A freedom sweet as ours.

Na de bevrijding
(Translated by James Brockway)

LOVE

In the Middle Ages, the love *motif* in Dutch literature formed the theme of many narrative and lyrical poems and of the drama. The narrative poems include the fine epic entitled 'Floris ende Blanchefloer', which relates the story of a Moorish prince, who traces his beloved to the harem of the Emir of Babylon and even succeeds in winning her from him. But the most remarkable feature is that even as early as 1360 or therebouts the love *motif* in the Southern Netherlands provided the inspiration for the composition of a number of highly original plays, and one of these—'Lanseloet'—a tragic play about immature love, is of particular importance as an early psychological approach.

Love as an archetypal human phenomenon belongs to all ages alike. The greatest Dutch lyrical poet was the son of a burgomaster of Amsterdam, one, Pieter Corneliszoon Hooft who lived from 1581 to 1647, and it was he who brought the love sonnet to perfection. An example of one of these sonnets follows:

My love, my love, thus spoke my love to me,
While on her delicate lips my lips were browsing.
Those words, too clear to be in need of glozing,
Entered my ears and stirred mysteriously
My inmost thoughts into tumultuous stress.
They did not trust the ear and at their pressure
I begged my dearest for a fuller measure
Of that confession, and she did confess.

Oh, bounty of the heart that overflows!
Entranced, each heart did th'other's heart imprison.
But when the morning star fled for the risen
Light of the sun, the sad truth too arose:
Oh, Gods, how close are things that are and seem!
How like the dream is life, like life the dream!

(Translated by Adriaan J. Barnouw)

With French classicism and the rationalism of the Enlightenment strongly dominant, the 18th century did not provide a favourable climate for the writing of love poetry, though the Netherlands, too, can provide a few examples of successful Arcadian poetry. Neither was the Romantic Movement, with its marked sentimentality, a suitable background for the expression of love. A fortunate exception was Staring, a gentleman farmer, who lived in Gelderland from 1767 to 1840, where he spent his life far removed from the culture of the big cities. Here is a love poem, as controlled as it is spontaneous.

RECOLLECTION

We sheltered under dripping willows,
Crouched by the water's edge.
The swallows skimmed the rippling billows
And played round silvery sedge.
Sweet fragrance carried on the breeze
Blew life into the willow trees.

The dripping ceased and stilled the shadows.
The birds had gone to rest.
The dew crept uphill from the meadows.
Light lingered in the west.
Then May burst into song, and we
Listened in silent ecstasy.

I looked at her in mute surrender
Of raptured soul to soul.
Her lovely eyes shone with a splendour,
Whose magic bound me whole.
Sweet whispering lips that felt the bliss,
And rendered it, of love's first kiss!

The willows decked us with their shadows,
Dusk fled on silent toes,
And darkness trailed across the meadows,
Reluctantly we rose.
Live long in memory, unforgot,   Herdenking
O, holy hour, O, sacred spot.   (Translated by Adriaan J. Barnouw)

21

In the art of the novel, which did not enter upon its period of full flowering until the end of the 18th century, love in all its aspects forms the indispensable theme, and the Netherlands is no exception in this respect. In the novel's early stages, the ruling morals of the time keep the sexual element within strict limits. When, however, about the year 1885 the influence of French Naturalism, and of Emile Zola in particular, begins to make itself felt in Holland, Dutch literature also goes much farther in this direction. In 1887 a novel, entitled 'Een Liefde' (A Love Affair), by a still very youthful author, Lodewijk van Deyssel (1864-1952), caused a great sensation. Since those days modern authors have been much more open-hearted. But there was also a reaction. A master like Arthur van Schendel (1874-1946) always observed classical limits, depicting love, and particularly its longing, in the form of the love-dream. His story 'Moonlight', from which the following excerpts have been taken, bears witness to this.

'The ship brought me to this town. I was not long in meeting young people here who were friends of mine and with whom I enjoyed myself a great deal, but I decided to stay here a few weeks only and then sail on further south with a fresh cargo. But the ship still lies at anchor in the roads and has sailed no more. At first I was merely loitering, but afterwards I could no longer leave the place. I had seen a girl here and was so utterly imbued with her loveliness that I knew before long that I was in love as few men ever are. Her father was a man of importance and there was not the slightest hope for me, not even of being able to speak to her. You know I'm no dreamer. I was resigned, therefore, because I knew that the insignificant must be modest in their desires. But I wanted at least to see her as much as I could, and consequently I would walk round and round her house late at night, wondering whether the small light that burned behind the window could be hers—I heard later that that *is* her room, where you can see the lighted window in the corner, to the left; the candle always burns there now, as soon as it grows dark.

You will understand why I always feel happiest, when the moon is shining as it is shining now. It was just such an evening. I searched in vain for a spot of shadow, dark enough to conceal my presence there in the roadway, for I was afraid of being seen. I stood watching, behind that hedge, there where you can see an opening in the twigs. The garden was

22

exactly the same as now, the same stocks were in bloom. They were so white that I could not help staring at them a long time. Imagine my emotion when, quite unexpectedly, I caught sight of her, sitting on this bench, dressed in a red gown, her face, like mine, turned towards the flowers. Oh, I've seen it all again so many times in my imagination, yet I can still feel the thumping of my heart...

I could not turn my eyes away. I can still recall quite clearly what my thoughts were: I was thinking whether that old man I heard shuffling behind me was really a living being or a phantom—a strange thought, don't you think? My emotions afterwards, however, were far stranger. The moon was shining even more brightly, more radiantly, than it is now. Lit by its gleam, her face was more adorable than I had ever seen it look before. She moved her head and I saw her eyes, dark and peaceful, turned towards me.

Neither of us moved. We remained staring at each other. I was seized by a sensation of calm joy, such as everyone feels at some time or other, a sensation that the supreme happiness that never quite becomes real is present, near at hand. She rose up from her bench, and with the train of her gown gathered up in her hand, walked through the field of flowers straight towards me. I did not know what was happening. She put her hand through the twigs and said: 'Come into the garden here. I've seen your face so often.' I climbed through the hedge and held her in my arms. Then we told each other our innermost thoughts. We spoke but few words and noticed that it had grown late, for the sounds had died away in the distance. I left her and returned homewards, filled with the shy wonder that you will know, if you have ever heard a woman say that she loves you. That was the sweetest night of my life.' Maneschijn

(Translated by James Brockway)

Modern poetry, like modern prose, is rich in love themes, though they seldom appear in isolation, being usually woven into a larger whole and related to all manner of other aspects of human experience. During the last century Dutch literature has produced no great poem devoted to glorifying the object of the poet's love, but it would be a simple ask to compile a lyrical anthology of a hundred excellent sonnets or strophic poems devoted to love or to the beloved. One of the poets included would undoubtedly be Bertus Aafjes, born in 1914, who wrote the following poem.

AMOROUS DITTY IN THE EARLY MORN

When in the early morning light,
Crouched by the fire, I'm moved to gaze
At my love, who tugs with lips set tight
At the strings and laces of her stays,

And see how her full, young bosom, white,
In that cruel confinement heaves and plays,
As though her heart must suffocate,
Pain quivers through me, secret, light,

To see such wild abundance dressed,
Such beauty in the busk compressed,
And I bless with trembling lips the sight,
The mist, the may, the morning light.

Amoureus liedje in den morgenstond
(Translated by James Brockway)

LAUGHTER

Laughter is one of the most real differences between man and the animals, and it is not surprising that the laughter-provoking situations which life treats us to now and again should have found their way into literature. One of the great poets of Holland's Golden Age was Bredero, to whom the Netherlands owe a number of imperishable comedies and farces, besides humorous songs on a par with the paintings of Jan Steen. In Bredero's works we find the life of the common people of his time, rough and exuberant as it was, faithfully depicted, as seen through the laughing eyes of a young artist who enjoys life in its every aspect. As a young citizen of Amsterdam, he looked upon the farmers and peasants from the villages surrounding the city with a certain scorn and disdain. But then, in Shakespeare, too, the peasants and menials provide the comic, ludicrous element. Here is a translation of one of Bredero's comic poems, depicting a peasants' party:

A PEASANTS' PARTY

Arnold Peter Gilson, and Matthew, Jack, and Jane,
And Nicholas and Colin, they sallied forth in train
To the village of Vinkeveen
For old Bill Bruce had given his goose
For the game of catch-the-crane.

Arnold Peter Gilson he had a stately gait.
His hat of velveteen stood pert upon his pate,
Aslant, and black as slate.
He wore it near across one ear.
It stood at half-past-eight.

But Matthew, and Janie, and Jack and Jock and Gene,
They were still-accoutred as their parents had been,
In red, in white, in green,
In greyish hue, in purple, in blue,
Like countryfolk, I mean.

Arrived in Vinkeveen, among the jostle and jam,
They found there Cornelius, and Tony and John Scram,
And Dirck of Diemerdam,
And Simon Sniff, and John the Stiff,
With Mat and Bernie Bam.

The girls from Vinkeveen and all that bailiwick,
My, how they'd polished their finest silver rig!
Oh boys, they looked so slick!
But fancy, Neltje had got her belt
From tall Matilda on tick!

They joined the company, and oh, the goings-on,
The drinking, the singing, the dancing and can-can,
The money lost and won.
They called for wine, that was in line.
Each bumpkin was a Don.

But Matthew and Katie, that sweet and simple lass,
These two sneaked together into the new-mown grass,
Not to say morning mass!
You know their game, it is ever the same.
I thought it was a farce.

Reckless Ernie Gilson was first to pull his jack
Against Peter Sorehead with many a hew and a hack.
And baldpate Brent came back
With a pitchfork dash, but got a gash
With others of his pack.

The lasses they beat it, not liking that debate.
There was a wild clatter of pewter, platter and plate.
But Colin he was great:
He slashed about, and killed a lout,
Who fell with cloven pate.

Simon seized the poker, and the settle of solid oak,
And flung them bang at Eben and at another bloke.
The missiles flew and broke
With might and main through panel and pane.
I left those crazy folk.

Ye gentlemen, ye burghers, who don't carouse and reel,
Shun the peasant's parties, they are never so genteel
But there is blood to spill.
Join me and mine in a jug of wine,
And steer an even keel.   Boeren-geselschap

(Translated by Adriaan J. Barnouw)

Towards the end of the 17th century wit became frozen under the influence of the correct and stiff propriety of the time.

A new form of wit develops, however, in the Romantic period, partly as a result of English influences. The cult of humour reaches a climax about the year 1840. Most of the authors at the time were theological students, and one collection of stories, the 'Camera Obscura' by Nicolaas Beets (1814-1903) achieved enormous popularity, mainly because of its realism and its depiction of the homeliness of the Dutch way of life. Shortly afterwards the influence of Heinrich Heine made itself felt in a student poet, who called himself Pieter Paaltjens and who acquired fame on account of one slim volume of poems entitled 'Sobs and Grins' (Snikken en Grimlachjes). Here is a lighthearted example of his humour:

TO RIKA

Once, only once, I saw your face. You were
Seated in the express that passed the train
In which I sat, so fast, so swift, I swear
So brief an encounter won't occur again.

And yet it lasted long enough to send
Me down life's weary path a lovelorn swain;
My smiling, carefree youth came to an end
The day I saw you seated in that train.

27

Why, tell me why, did you have such light-brown hair?
The hair men recognize angels by—and then
Why were your eyes so blue? Why? Was that fair?
You knew their power to spellbind this poor man.

And why rush past, without a backward look?
Why did you not, like lightning, turn and race
Down the train and fling your arms around my neck
And press hot lips to mine in fierce embrace?

Afraid, perhaps, you'd cause the trains to crash?
But, RIKA, could I greater joy attain
Than in the hellish rattle and the clash,
To be crushed to death with you by the self-same train?

By the year 1890 the 19th century cult of humour seemed to have
been exhausted in the Netherlands, and in the first quarter of the 20th
century there were only a few writers who now and again turned out a
humorous piece of prose or a comic verse. The revival dates from around
the year 1930, while after World War II humour in fact became a
fashion. Simon Carmiggelt (born in 1913), in particular, has acquired a
great reputation with many collections of short stories and sketches which
bear witness to unusual powers of observation, great intuition and, above
all, to a subtle feeling for words. Modern humour amounts, in fact, to a play
on words as well as a game with life, and it is precisely here that Carmiggelt
is a master. His success has a social and psychological side to it as well—
the smile he conjures up in depicting all manner of everyday scenes acts
as a consolation for the threats which oppress postwar man. Here is a brief
sketch, typical of Carmiggelt's humour:

LANTERN SLIDES

The gentleman from Edam had made a trip to Australia, and since he
couldn't resist telling us about it, he delivered the inevitable lecture with
the inevitable lantern slides in one of those small and unutterably dismal
little halls no single town is without. Apart from four members of the
committee of the society which organized his lecture, there were present

a bevy of elderly young ladies, together with two immaculately attired clerks and a greybeard, who probably had a nephew in Sydney anyway. Of the three reporters who beguiled their time saying rude things about the lecturer I will say nothing. I should, however, draw your attention to the magic lantern, which stood at the rear of the hall, at its side a small box of glass slides and a young man in spectacles, looking as though he would at any moment burst into tears.

In his opening address, the chairman of the society expressed his disappointment and distress at the absence of the members, discerning in the attitude of reserve they had thus chosen to adopt towards the speaker —and, indeed, towards an entire continent—some highly ulterior motive.

The globe-trotter himself, small and bald-headed, belonged to that ineradicable tribe of orators who insist on making speeches, though entirely devoid of oratorical ability. With the diction of a chemist, he read out from a disturbingly tall pile of notes, covered, every inch of them, with minute handwriting. This system has the drawback of being tiresome, but the saving grace of enabling one to see, from the height of the pile, how long the agony is still to go on for.

On this occasion it went on for a very long time, because, before broaching the subject proper, the orator became involved in the most elaborate observations on travel in general, and on his own cunning ruses in particular. When he had made it sufficiently clear to us that he was not the sort to allow any race or nation to get the better of him, the moment approached for him to have the lights extinguished so as to make a beginning with the slides.

'And here, ladies and gentlemen, is a portrait of Dr. March, my excellent host in Sydney, to whom I am so deeply indebted for his kind assistance and advice,' read out the gentleman from Edam, whereupon he rapped on his desk with his little pencil. This noise had no significant effect: no slide appeared in the circle of white light on the screen. The orator looked up from his papers, sent a piercing glance into the pervading gloom, and spoke: 'Slide!'

At this, the young gentleman with the spectacles stood up in the second row and stumbled his way to his post. That he had arrived at his destination was made obvious a moment or two later by a sudden sideways swing of the circle of white light, which now come to rest upon the lecturer himself. Such things can happen. The technical expert was not slow in detecting his error and swung the lantern back into its original position. The speaker bent down over his notes once again and repeated: 'And here, ladies and gentlemen, is a portrait of Dr. March, my excellent host in Sydney, to whom I am so deeply indebted for his kind assistance and advice'. Now a slide was, indeed, slid into the machine. On the screen appeared the branch of a tree, from which was suspended, remarkably enough, a plump little bear, who stared at us all with a look of entirely unjustified arrogance. There was a muttering in the audience, for it was difficult to believe that in Australia little bears of this kind are awarded doctors' degrees.

When the speaker saw the small animal appear on the screen, his face assumed the expression of one caught in a snare. He clawed impotently at the air, as though desirous of preventing what had already happened. 'This slide comes later on', he stuttered. The little bear was now whisked away beyond the range of our vision, to be replaced a moment later by the image of an aborigine, in little more than his birthday suit, and reclining on a staff. To add a touch of liveliness, the technical gentleman had inserted this slide upside down.

While the audience were asking themselves what the slide was actually meant to represent, the speaker had left his desk. He joined his 'assistant', engaged in a whispered exchange of views with him, and returned to the rostrum. Once again the circle of white light appeared on the screen, and in this circle the portrait of a grey-haired gentleman did, indeed, become visible. 'And here, ladies and gentlemen, is a portrait...' the orator began nervously.

Then the magic lantern fell over.

Lichtbeelden
(Translated by James Brockway)

RELIGION

In the Middle Ages the Church exercised a deep influence on society and the whole culture of the time was impregnated with the Christian faith. The various religious festivals, Christmas, Good Friday and Easter particularly, spoke to the imagination of believers, who, unable to read and write themselves, got their religion by word of mouth from Bible stories, the lives of the saints, accounts of miracles, and from sermons. The figure of the Virgin Mary played a highly important role and countless are the legends woven round her in the Middle Ages. One of the finest of these is the legend of Beatrice, a nun who deserts her convent for profane love and who is redeemed by the Virgin's loving mercy. This narrative poem, as simple as it is moving, represents one of the peak achievements of medieval literature in the Lowlands. Countless, too, are the sacred songs and carols on the theme of Christmas and the Three Kings. They display a simple faith in God, while their authors seem to be on good, one might even say familiar, terms with the divine personages of whom they sing. Here is a translation of one of these anonymous poems:

THE THREE KINGS

Here we come with our bright star,
We seek the Lord Jesus, we come from afar.
We came and knocked at Herod's door.
Herod himself he opened the door,
Herod, with wicked heart, he spoke:
Why is the youngest of three so black?
He is black, indeed, but wide his fame,
A king, and from the Orient came.
We came and climbed upon a hill,
There we saw the star stand still.
O star! do not stand still, we pray!
To Bethlehem show us the way.
At Bethlehem, in that fair town,
Mary with her child we found.
The smaller child, the greater God!
A Happy New Year we pray from God.

Drie koningen leys   (Translated by Adriaan J. Barnouw)

31

The Reformation had a decisive influence in the Netherlands. Calvinism set its stamp on the second half of the 16th and the whole of the 17th century, though other forms of Christian belief were winked at. Great toleration must have been shown, otherwise it would not have been possible for Vondel to have become so important a figure in the life of the time. He was first a Mennonite, later a Catholic, and openly anti-Calvinist all his life. Vondel is the poet of the classic biblical drama, employing themes derived from the Old Testament. In some of his dramas, such as 'Lucifer' and 'Adam in Exile', his work is on a level with the finest achievements of world literature. Among sacred songs his 'Hymn to the Godhead' has never been surpassed. But in his more intimate poetry, too, he showed a continuous awareness of man's dependence on God.

During the greater part of the 18th century a rational Christianity held sway for the most part in the Netherlands, a Christianity which appealed to the mind rather than to the heart. The Romantic Movement restored religion to its former place—to being an affair of the emotions. Willem Bilderdijk, a poet who came forward as a fiery champion of Calvinism, lived from 1756 to 1831. Much of his poetry has become entirely outmoded owing to its rhetoric. Now and again, however, a poem of his has retained its emotional power, thanks to the personal note he has succeeded in giving it. For example, this prayer:

PRAYER

Merciful God, who readst my inmost mind,
I flee to Thee, and would, but cannot pray.
Behold my downcast spirit, my eyes purblind
With streaming tears no soothing words can stay.

I do not ask for aught, a broken reed.
My baffled senses grip me in their hold.
Thou alone knowest what Thy child does need.
Thy love exceeds his self-love, thousandfold.

To Thine unknowing son make up his loss.
He dares not ask for aught, nor even knows.
I bow me down, beg neither cure nor cross.
Do as Thy infinite mercy may dispose.

"Muiderslot",
where P. C. Hooft lived for
38 years.
17th century engraving.

Pieter Corneliszoon Hooft
(1581-1647)

Guido Gezelle (1830-1899)

Yea, wound or heel, raise up or down my mind.
I shall adore Thy will, dark though it be.
I offer up myself, still and resigned.
All that I ask for is to rest in Thee.

I look to Thee in awe, like children may,
With Christian hope no petulance impairs.
O teach me God, what Thou wilt have me pray.
Pray Thou Thyself in me and cleanse my prayers.   Gebed

(Translated by Adriaan J. Barnouw)

A far greater poet than Bilderdijk is the Flemish priest, Guido Gezelle (1830-1899). It is difficult to say whether Gezelle is a modern or a man of the Middle Ages. Living in 19th century Flanders, where nothing had changed for centuries, Gezelle seemed to resurrect the ancient spirit of Gothic times. Yet at the same time his poetry is modern, being extremely individual in its use of language, and displaying a sensitivity to nature which one finds nowhere else in Dutch literature. He sees God's creative power in a flowering plant or singing bird, discerns the Eternal in the smaller things of life. Yet there were also periods of tension in his life, of misjudgement and tragic grief. One feels this in the following poem, another prayer, but so much more charged with emotion than Bilderdijk's.

YOU PRAYED ON THE MOUNTAINSIDE, ALONE

You prayed on the mountainside, alone,
but ... Jesu, there's no mountain, none,
high enough where I can climb
and find you there, alone:
the world pursues, wherever I
go or turn or cast my eye;
and poor as I am there is none,
not one
who's needy and cannot complain;
hungry, and cannot beg; whom pain
tortures, and he cannot say
how bitterly!   Gij badt op eenen berg alleen
O, teach this idiot, teach him how to pray!

(Translated by James Brockway)

33

From the 19th century onwards apostasy, the exodus from the church, has been on the increase in the Netherlands. Christian belief is no longer a matter of course and there are scores whose writing is inspired by religious scepticism. The Flemish novelist Gerard Walschap, born in 1898, was originally a Catholic but went over later in life to a free-thinking, secular humanism. Faith is still often present, as a problem, in his work, and in a splendid novel entitled 'The Treatment of Christ' he has set off the religious ecstasy of the simple believer against the scepticism of the intellectual personified in the figure of Asver, a rich landowner at the time of the birth of Jesus. The following fragment gives an impression of this. It is the day after Jesus was born:

'Asver accompanied them. On the way they told him what had happened. Most of them had been sleeping, but not John and Pancras. 'Why did they keep watch with you?' Asver asked. They did not know. John had been the first to hear it, a strange music, and averred that it was approaching them, but coming, not from the distance, but from above. Pancras then looked up at the sky and saw a small, faint spot, which descended above their heads, grew bigger and spread out to become a blinding circle of light. Then he was sore afraid and shouted to the others to wake up.

The music was now coming from quite close by. They could clearly discern, in their own language and dialect, the words: 'Glory to God in the highest and on earth peace to men of goodwill'. They sprang up. The ring of light circled around them and in that ring of light they could see angels standing. No, my lord, not people, angels, say what you will! Above their heads there'd come a voice: 'Shepherds, I bring you tidings of great joy which shall be to all people. For unto you this night a Saviour, Christ the Lord, is born. Ye shall find a babe wrapped in swaddling clothes, lying in a lowly stable. And this shall be a sign unto you.'

Suddenly everything had vanished, and when they looked up they saw that all cows, oxen and sheep had fled, but that all the lambs in their fold were standing, huddled closely together in a perfect circle, and bleating, staring at the spot where the light had vanished.

Blind John took hold of Pancras by the hand and called to the others: 'Follow us!' They followed after him. He leapt over ditch and canal, avoiding every obstacle, without anyone to guide or warn him. 'Let us make for that tall poplar', he said. 'From there we shall see the star'. No one understood a word of what he was saying. They went, oppressed by all manner of fears, and at times they could not hold back a cry. Arrived at the poplar, John stood still, pointed a finger skywards and inquired of them whether they could not see the star there. No, they couldn't. 'There!' he pointed, 'just between those two pines, a little nearer the one on the left, and just above it'. And it was true. They saw it now. There it was, a great glittering star, very low in the sky and travelling ahead of them.

'Where?' Asver asked. 'There, master'. He could not see it and gave a laugh.

He let them continue with their story. When they arrived at the little stable, he chuckled: 'Now let me see him, this famous Messiah of yours. But what right had he to take possession of one of my cattle pens?'

He stepped inside. In one corner he saw the carpenter who had solicited for work through John, a pot of water hanging over a fire and, beside it, old Pancras, down on his knees and blowing at the flames. Next to him sat another of his servants, weaving a wicker cradle. Somewhere in another corner someone was playing sweetly on a reed pipe. For the rest everything was so quiet and so dark that Asver could distinguish nothing clearly. No one stood up for him, no one made way for him, no one stirred. Whereas, when he appeared at the gateway of his farm, all his servants, as far as eye could see, would be filled with fear and awe of him, here it was just as though his presence had gone unnoticed. Then he spoke in a loud and harsh voice. 'Open the door and make light! I want to be able to see your Messiah'. A gust of icy wind and a splash of light entered the stable, and now, in the centre of it, Asver could see a frail young woman, still a child, bent over an old manger, its edges nibbled away by the beasts. In it lay a newborn babe with nothing at all remarkable about it, as far as Asver could detect. Around the manger six of his shepherds were kneeling in prayer, their rugged faces almost touching the ground, an attitude of reverence too much like that cringeing awe he despised in others for Asver's liking. Leaning against the doorpost, stood John, the blind cowherd, playing on his reed pipe with an indescribable purity and clarity of tone, and letting his tears and the chilly bubbles that formed on the tip of his nose drip down, unheeded, onto his hands and tight jacket. His miserable sticks of legs shivered in his scanty breeches, but his blind, hollow eyes were fixed on heaven in unutterable ecstasy. He, the image of poverty and need, to whom God's infinite love had been revealed, could not relieve his overburdened heart, pipe as he would! Listening to him, the shepherds were at times so overcome with joy that they would lie stretched out prone on the mud floor, and sob quietly. But Asver, their lord and master, stood there, baffled and aghast. Impotent rage began to surge deep within him, like the lava in a volcano that has slept for centuries. He saw what he was up against: the stubborn hunger for the fairytale, the obscure hankering after mystery, in defiance of fact and reality. A child as poor as a church mouse, a perfectly ordinary child in a stable. And precisely because there was nothing to justify their belief, they believed!'

      Bejegening van Christus   (Translated by James Brockway)

Despite widespread scepticism, religious conviction still inspires many a Dutch poet to write poems. Here is an English rendering of a poem by Martinus Nijhoff, who died in 1953.

THE SOLDIER WHO CRUCIFIED CHRIST

We nailed him to the cross. His fingers bled,
Clutched wildly at the nail, as I raised the hammer—
But, gently, his voice pronounced my name; he said:
'Love me'—and his secret was mine for ever.

I twist back a laugh, my teeth I grit,
I become a madman, demanding blood of love:
I love him—and I smite and smite and smite,
And drive the nail home till the timber's split.

Now, like a fool, a nail through my own palm,
I trace a fish—his name, his monogram—
On every wall I find, on every beam and tree,
Or in my breast, or, crouching, in the sand.

And answer those who stop and question me:
'He took a nail and drove it through my hand'.

      De soldaat die Jezus kruisigde   (Translated by James Brockway)

DEATH

Throughout Europe the later Middle Ages were a period of trial and terror in many guises. The lives of simple citizens and farmers were constantly threatened by strife between princes and petty rulers, but even worse was the scourge of epidemics which could wipe out half the inhabitants of a town in a matter of weeks. The plague, cholera, smallpox kept the people of medieval times in a state of terror, and probably at no other period in his history has man been made so conscious of his mortality. This is apparent from the celebrated Dances of Death, homilies in the form of woodcuts accompanied by texts, in which Death appears as the Great Leveller who respects neither emperors nor popes, children nor lovers. It is to this death theme that the Netherlands owes its world-famous morality 'Elckerlijc' (Everyman), written about the year 1500 by a Flemish author, Petrus van Diest. This play has since become part of the international theatrical repertoire in the form of an early English adaptation and a modern German version by the poet Hugo von Hofmannsthal. It is a tense and gripping drama in which the main character, Everyman, is warned to make his peace with God, for he has to set out on a long journey on which there can be no turning back. Everything and everyone he had counted upon fall away from him at the critical moment, so that he is finally left with only Virtue, fortified by Confession. Thus reconciled with God, Elckerlijc dies and his soul is conveyed to heaven by the angels. Elckerlijc * is an arresting drama, of wide human appeal, that deserves the place it still holds on the stage.

Death is something more, however, than a great and anonymous force of general significance. It is also a factor which intervenes intimately and directly in the personal life of everyone of us, by removing our parents, our friends, and sometimes our children. Among the poems that the Middle Ages have handed down to us, there is one death-lament that strikes so direct, so personal, a note, that one still feels its author's grief, five or six centuries after it was written. It is a poem of 19 lines, based on two rhymes and entitled: 'Egidius, waer bestu bleven?'—Egidius, where are you hiding?

* Pronounced Elckerlyc.

EGIDIUS, WHERE ARE THOU HIDING?

Egidius, where are you hiding?
I long for you, companion mine;
You died, you left me here abiding:
How sweet was life, when we were twain.
It seemed there could be no dividing,
Yet now you stand beside God's throne,
More radiant than the high sun riding,
All joys, all riches now are thine.

Egidius, where are you hiding?
I long for you, companion mine;
You died, you left me here abiding.

Now pray for me, who, here abiding,
Must suffer still the cold world's pain.
Keep me a place, a place beside thee—
I've yet to sing a brief refrain,
Till Death doth make us one again.
Egidius, where are you hiding?
I long for you, companion mine;
You died, you left me here abiding.   Egidius, waer bestu bleven?

(Translated by James Brockway)

During the 17th century poems of death in Dutch literature took on a distinctly more social note, the death of an important person providing the occasion for countless poets to write memorial lines. Vondel's work contains a whole series of such poems, dedicated to princes of the House of Orange, naval heroes, mayors of Amsterdam, personal friends and also to his own children. Of these he had four but lost the youngest, Constantijn, and the youngest but one, his eight-year-old daughter, Saartje, the one child shortly after the other. These poems are charged with true paternal emotion and the latter, especially, is highly moving. Entitled 'Uitvaert van mijn Dochterken'—My Daughter Departing...—it achieves a tender pathos with its straightforward description of the games and pastimes of childhood, so that the little girl comes wholly to life for us. The poem is

human, of this world, and makes a more direct appeal to us today than much
of Vondel's other work. Here are its opening lines.

MY DAUGHTER DEPARTING....

Fell Death, who Youth, who Joy, cannot behold,
Reprieves the grey and old.
On high She sits and aims her cruel dart
At the poor mite's heart.
And laughs, when taking leave,
Fond mothers weep and grieve.
A babe She spied, that, fleet and free from care,
Was loved by all, and everywhere
She came; who danced and nimble-footed skipped,
And sang her songs and tripped
In Ring a ring o' roses,
A pocket full of posies,
Or, followed by a lively, raucous troop,
Pursued the rattling hoop
Through street and lane, sprang, laughing, on the swing,
Or played at housekeeping
(The prelude to the days
That banish childhood's joys),
Or was bold to see, when dibs was played,
The children's law obeyed,
Rolling and snatching, on the leaping ivory bone,
The knuckles from the stone
And lived the life enchanted,
By gold nor chattels haunted ...   Uitvaert van mijn dochterken
                                          (Translated by James Brockway)

The Romantic period produced many verses by poets of melancholy
bent in which the transitoriness of human existence was described with
emphasis and great elaboration.

For the man of modern times death has taken on an entirely different
aspect—though its mystery and inevitability remain. P. N. van Eyck, who
was born in 1887 and died in 1954, has described its mystery in a poem of

39

four quatrains entitled 'Oh, Death, Mysterious Nightingale', in which death is represented by the fascinating and original image of the nightingale, singing in the darkness of the wood and enticing man along its mossy paths away from the lighted cities of life. Its inevitability he has depicted in one of the best-known of 20th century Dutch poems, 'De Tuinman en de Dood'—The Gardener and Death.

THE GARDENER AND DEATH

This morning, pale, aghast, my gardener ran
Into my house: Master, I must be gone!

I was working, pruning roses, unaware,
And there stood Death and fixed me with his stare.

Afraid, I dashed away as fast as could be,
Yet saw him raise his hand and threaten me.

My lord, your horse, your spurs, let me be gone.
Before nightfall I'll be in Ispahan!

Long had he fled, and as the day grew dark,
Death I encountered in the cedar park.

Why, I demand (for he waits and no word will he say)
Did you threaten my gardener earlier today?

Smiling, he makes reply: My gesture meant
No threat to him; it was astonishment

To find him working here this morn, the man
Whom I must seize tonight in Ispahan.   De tuinman en de dood
(Translated by James Brockway)

Van Eyck is not the only poet to have been so vividly aware of the oppressiveness of death. The Flemish poet, Karel van de Woestijne (1878-1929), who also has a number of prose works to his credit, wrote an impressive short novel, entitled 'The Farmer Who Dies' (De boer die sterft), which has been referred to, not without justice, as a modern Elckerlijc. The poet E. du Perron was also deeply disturbed by the same theme, as is witnessed by his poem 'Prayer to Obdurate Death' (Gebed tot de harde dood), and likewise his contemporary, H. Marsman (1899-1940), whose work contains a volume, 'Porta Nigra', which is dominated from beginning to end by the theme of death. But among modern Dutch poets it is Gerrit Achterberg of whom one inevitably thinks in this connection. One of the most famous and original of contemporary Dutch poets, Achterberg, who lived from 1905 to 1962, was deeply concerned, haunted in fact, by the theme of death. It has been said of his work that it amounts to a mystical-magical attempt to exorcise death, a desperate, but wholly serious, attempt to deny its existence. His loved one is dead—but she exists everywhere in the world around him—she has become part of the matter which makes up the objects of everyday life—and he seeks to reach her through the mystical agency of words become poems. Here is one of his poems. 'Divining Rod', which is highly characteristic of his poetry both in form and subject matter.

DIVINING ROD

You have made yourself a part of that
Which men call 'world', my habitat;
Needle in a haystack which I find
At every point where I admit
A poem to life: oh, you are not
Hidden from my eyes, my hands,
Staring, I grope for you through the brands,
The fires of matter, to isolate
You from Creation: whole, complete.   Wichelroede

(Translated by James Brockway)

Existentialism, in which death and the immaterial are important factors in human existence, has had a powerful influence on a number of contemporary Dutch authors. It is not surprising, therefore, that a woman novelist like Anna Blaman, who won fame in the post-war period and who died suddenly in 1960, should have frequently returned to this theme in her novels and stories. She devoted one of her more recent books, the novel

'A Matter of Life and Death', to the acceptance of dying as a personal problem. Here is an extract from that novel. In it the main character, a heart patient like Anna Blaman herself, is speaking:

'It was not that anything shrivelled inside me; but love and friendship, and every other ideal emotion, were gradually decaying like necrotic tissues. I was left with nothing. I felt lost and shut out. There was no mortal soul I could tell that my heart was beginning to toll like a death-bell, no mortal soul to whom I could tell that, without appealing to his generosity and his pity. And the more I longed to be able to tell, the more fiercely my pride resisted the idea. And to deliver up my pride in its death struggle, now especially in its death struggle, was more than I had the heart—an abandoned, sick heart—to do.

I once knew a man whose wife was seriously ill. He would come to the newspaper office, distracted, and tell everybody, literally everybody willing to listen to him: 'My wife is ill. How it will all end...' And everyone said: 'How awful for you. But let's hope for the best.' A little later: 'She gets thinner every day. She's in unbearable pain. God only knows what it is.' And everyone said: 'Keep on hoping. Where there's life, there's hope.'

Later still: 'I know now what it is, but she doesn't. So you'll understand...'

Later still: 'It can't possibly last much longer.'

And then: 'It's over.'

And everyone expressed their sympathy with him, for he had involved everyone in his drama... and why not? Everyone of us bears the same death within him, and when the moment comes, he will stir in you, too, striking slowly or swiftly. He will creep like poison through your blood, insinuate himself into your heart, your kidneys, your lungs and your brain, and soon he will stretch himself out in your four limbt in rigid ease.'

Op leven en dood
(Translated by James Brockway)

THE MOTHERLAND

No country in Europe has a national anthem as old as the Wilhelmus, the national anthem of Holland. It was written by an anonymous author about the year 1570, during the early stages of the rising against Spain, when the Prince of Orange had suffered a number of defeats in minor battles and had been obliged to withdraw for the time being to his domains in Germany. Taking the form of an address by the Prince to his followers, the anthem consists of no less than fifteen verses, the first letters of which spell the Prince's name, Willem van Nassau. It is one of the most arresting historical poems in Dutch literature, and perhaps in world literature, too. Here follow some verses, containing the famous lines which give expression to the freedom of conscience that the Netherlands acquired so early on in their history.

WILLIAM OF NASSAU

William of Nassau, scion
Of a Dutch and ancient line,
I dedicate undying
Faith to this land of mine.
A prince I am, undaunted,
Of Orange, ever free.
To the King of Spain I've granted
A lifelong loyalty.

A shield and my reliance,
O God, Thou ever wert.
I'll trust unto Thy guidance,
O leave me not ungirt,
That I may stay a pious
Servant of Thine for aye,
And drive the plagues that try us
And tyranny away.

Nothing so moves my pity
As seeing through these lands

Field, village, town and city
Pillaged by roving bands.
O that the Spaniards rape thee,
My Netherland so sweet,
The thought of that doth grip me,
Causing my heart to bleed.

Unto the Lord His Power
I do confession make
That ne'er at any hour
Ill of the King I spake.
But unto God, the greatest
Of Majesties, I owe
Obedience first and latest,
For Justice wills it so.   Wilhelmus van Nassaue
                                      (Translated by Adriaan J. Barnouw)

As far as the poets were concerned, the history of the Netherlands was for long mainly regional history. True national conciousness was slow to develop and was, in a sense, a typical feature of the Romantic Period. The 19th century poet, Bilderdijk, harboured strong, patriotic sentiments but expressed them in heavily overdone rhetoric. The Amsterdam poet, Helmers, went even further, composing a great, but bragging, poem during the days of French rule, entitled 'The Dutch Nation'. Potgieter, who lived from 1808 to 1875, and who, while travelling abroad as a young merchant, had learnt to appreciate Holland's special significance in Europe, wrote a shorter and far sincerer poem in praise of his country even though its rhetoric and rhythm may seem overdone to us today. It dates from the days of tension, when Belgium drew away from Holland and became a separate state in the year 1830. Here is Potgieter's poem:

HOLLAND

Grey are your heavens and stormy your strand,
Naked your dunes and unrimpled your meadows,
By Nature rough-hewn with a stepmother's hand,
Yet dearly, full-dearly, I love you, my land.

All that you are is our forefathers' work,
A miracle wrought by the toil of those heroes,
Too bold for the sea, for the tyrant a Turk,
Your freedom a temple, your piety a kirk.

Remain what you were when you bloomed like a flower,
That Europe may name you the homeland of order,
The oppressed may acclaim you, his refuge and bower,
Land of my Fathers, the land I adore.

And whate'er in the womb of the future lie curled,
Whate'er may await us, around your bright sword
And its unsullied blade, let green laurels be furled,
Land once the free'st, the most bless'd in the world.   Holland
(Translated by James Brockway)

Listen now to a very different voice, giving a very different picture of Holland. It is the voice of De Genestet, a younger contemporary of Potgieter's. De Genestet suffered severely as a result of the Dutch climate, far more severely than one would surmise from the jesting note in the following poem. It is a brief but justly deserved satire on the sentimentality and rhetoric that were all too evident in the patriotic poetry of the time.

SUCH IS HOLLAND

O, land of mud and mist, where man is wet and shivers,
Soaked with humidity, with damp and chilly dew,
O, land of unplumbed bogs, of roads resembling rivers,
Land of umbrellas, gout, colds, agues, toothache, 'flu.
O, spongy porridge-swamp, O, homeland of galoshes,
Of cobblers, toads, and frogs, peat-diggers, mildew, mould,
Of ducks and every bird that slobbers, splutters, splashes,
Hear the autumnal plaint of a poet with a cold!
Thanks to your clammy clime my arteries are clotted
With blood turned mud. No song, no joy, no peace for me.
You're fit for clogs alone, O, land our forebears plotted
And, not at my request, extorted from the sea.   Boutade
(Translated by Adriaan J. Barnouw)

45

There is a pronounced cosmopolitan note in more recent Dutch literature. No Dutchman still believes in the absolute independence of his small country, nor in its superiority. Yet, as Vondel wrote, 'Love of the Motherland is born in each man's breast', and the history of the last half century has made every Dutchman realize once more that there are certain advantages in belonging to our small nation, advantages which cannot be estimated too highly. Not intellectual or political advantages, but simpler things to do with everyday life. The leading ideas in the poetry of P. C. Boutens, who lived from 1870 to 1943, were drawn mainly from Plato. Yet in the impressive world of thought and feeling which Boutens' poetic gift constructed out of these themes, we suddenly come across a simple, lyrical poem which tells how conscious the poet was of the native scene and its significance to him as a source of inspiration.

HEART AND COUNTRY

Content my heart found nowhere,
Nowhere tranquillity,
But here, between your rivers,
Beside your giant sea,
My heart's green homeland, broad and free,
More real than life and death to me.

The wind sang through the trees and
Entered my silent door,
The voices of your streams and
Your sea's full-throated roar:
And then my heart burst into song,
My blood itself found words to sing.

All that I had to give men
You first had given me;
I sang of death, of living,
Of love's sweet agony:
The tenderest sigh from lover wrung
I turned to words in your own tongue.

46

More wonders, richer, stranger,
Your voice sings in my ear ...
May I, when Death must claim me,
Still hear your quickening choir!
Let but the wind Death's office do,
My heart shall welcome the adieu.

Hart en land
(Translated by James Brockway)

Boutens was not the only one to become more deeply aware of his nationality in the inter-war period. The entire younger generation, which was cosmopolitan in its outlook in 1920, became more conscious of being Dutch after 1933, when Nazi Germany began to threaten the whole of Europe and to flout the finest traditions which the Dutch nation had long upheld. A prominent figure among the writers of this new generation was H. Marsman, who lived from 1899 to 1940, and who wrote the following lines on Holland during a prolonged stay in France.

THINKING OF HOLLAND
Thinking of Holland,
I see broad rivers
languidly winding
through endless fen,
lines of incredibly
tenuous poplars
like giant plumes
on the polder's rim;
and sunk in tremendous,
open expanses,
the farmsteads scattered
across the plain,
coppices, hamlets,
squat towers and churches,
and elms composing
a proud domain.
Low leans the sky
and slowly the sun

47

in mists of mother-
of-pearl grows blurred,
and far and wide
the voice of the water,
of endless disaster
is feared and heard.

Herinnering aan Holland
(Translated by James Brockway)

How right the poem's last lines were was demonstrated by the great floods which swept over the Netherlands in February, 1953, costing nearly two thousand lives. It is as though Marsman had foreseen this disaster, just as, in another poem, he seems to have foreseen his own tragic end in June, 1940, when the boat on which he was trying to escape from France was torpedoed and sunk.

It goes without saying that the five years of the German occupation, from 1940 to 1945, stirred patriotic feelings in the Dutchman's breast. Some idea of the circumstances that reigned during those years has been given to the world by translations of Anne Frank's famous diary, in book form and also as a play. There is a critical streak in the Dutch character that delights in attacking what it loves truly and well; and then there is also the wish to avoid at all costs any display of the emotions. But just how deeply-rooted love of the mother country is in Dutch hearts can be seen whenever Dutchmen abroad are gathered and the Wilhelmus happens to be played.

AMSTERDAM

Compared with Athens, Rome and even London, Amsterdam is a relatively young city. In the Middle Ages it was still only a small fishing village, lying on the mouth of a small river, the River Amstel. During the 16th century, however, Amstelredam, as the city used to be called, began to expand so rapidly that by the next century, Holland's Golden Age, it had become the largest, richest and most influential city in the country and one of the leading ports of Europe and the world. It was also a centre of new ideas, of freedom of thought and religion, and of rich intellectual activity, the city of such poets as Hooft and Vondel, of the painter Rembrandt, the philosopher Spinoza.

Here are some lines of the great 17th century poet, Vondel, singing Amsterdam's praise at the height of her glory.

ON AMSTELREDAM

On the Amstel, on the waters, she stands, resplendent town,
She who as Empress wears proud Europe's shining crown!
Amstelredam, who lifts her brow to heaven's arches
And shoots, on Pluto's breast, her long roots through the marshes.
What waters have not borne the shadow of her sails?
What markets have not seen her wares burst from the bales?
What race beneath the moon knows not her lips' decrees,
She, who herself prescribes the law to the Seven Seas?
She spreads her pinions wide, by rich increase of souls,
And tugs the world inside, in overflowing hulls.
Prosperity shall be hers, if her Council, bold and wise,
Keep the Clergy in their place and their bandage from its eyes.

Op Amstelredam
(Translated by James Brockway)

It was during this period that the old centre of Amsterdam which we know today began to take shape: that the series of concentric, semi-circular canals were dug and lined by the tall and stately houses of the rich merchants who ruled the city, economically and politically. The Amsterdam of this period must have made an unforgettable impression on visitors, both by reason of its architecture and the life of its people. Constantijn Huygens, a contemporary of Vondel's, had travelled far and wide as a diplomat and knew such cities as Venice and London. Born and bred in The Hague, he must also have been conscious of the great difference—not to say antagonism—that has always existed between The Hague and Amsterdam. Yet, when in one of his 'Towns with Voices' poems, Huygens makes Amsterdam speak of herself, it is in the following way:

AMSTERDAM SPEAKS

My marvels do deserve a more than common awe.
The stranger ought to faint who came to see and saw
And, having seen, should say, 'How broughtst thou all the powers
Of all that's wonderful within thy moats and towers?
O, golden swamp, with heaven's plenitude replete,
Storehouse of East and West, all water and all street,
Twice-Venice, where's the end of the walls that embrace thee?'
But, stranger, speak not thus. Better in silence face me.
Praise Rome, praise Paris, praise Cairo's pageantry.
Who stands in silenced awe has spoken best of me.

Amsteldam
(Translated by Adriaan J. Barnouw)

Whereas in the days of her early blossoming, Amsterdam had been a centre of new ideas and great creative activity, in the 18th century life there took on a quieter air. It was not until after the Napoleonic era, and in the second half of the 19th century particularly, that the city began to expand once more. Numerous, not always very attractive, new quarters were built, though the beautiful old centre was preserved and has remained largely intact to our day. Yet even in these drab newer quarters, the inimitable spirit of Amsterdam makes itself felt, and we find an echo of this in a sonnet by J. C. Bloem, one of the finest and best-known of the older generation of contemporary Dutch poets. The poem is entitled 'De Dapperstraat' in Dutch, which means: Dapper Street. Dapper does not mean the same in Dutch as it does in English; it is simply the name of a man the street was called after. Everyone knows, however, that Dapper Street is a rather dull street in a poorer quarter of the city.

DAPPER STREET

Nature is for the empty, the contented—
And then, what can we boast of in this land?
A hill with a few small villas set against it,
A patch of wood no bigger than your hand.

Give me instead the sombre city highways,
The waterfront hemmed in between the quays,
Clouds reflected in an attic window—
Were ever clouds more beautiful than these?

All things are riches to the unexpectant—
Life holds her wonders hidden from our sight,
Then suddenly reveals them to perfection.
I thought this over, walking through the sleet,
The city grime, one grey and drizzly morning,
Blissfully happy, drenched in Dapper Street.   De Dapperstraat
                                              (Translated by James Brockway)

Amsterdam had also been a source of inspiration to Dutch prose writers and has provided many a novelist with the background for his novel. One of Holland's foremost modern novelists, F. Bordewijk, set one his books, entitled 'Blossoming Branch', in the city. In the following excerpt from that novel, the author describes a walk through one of the older and now largely deserted parts, the picturesque harbour quarter, known as the Western Islands.

'It was still December when they went out one Sunday morning for a walk with the children. They did this several times a year, allowing the children to choose the route they were to follow. In this way they got to know the city, both the newer and the older districts.

His wife, Aurora, was far less interested than van Marle himself was in the individual character of each of the different quarters, but she enjoyed the walk all the same, and on a windstill morning such as this, with the sky overcast, the city looked at its very loveliest. And then, as the wife of an architect, she had come with the years to realize how thrilling it was to live in a big city, in this one especially, if only one used one's eyes.

51

The houses and streets seemed to undergo sudden transformations, due to changes in the light or to the changing moods of the observer. There were more gradual changes, too, coming about subtly, smoothly, yet inevitably, due to the corrosion of the atmosphere, and due as well to the corrosion of the human being whose eyes observed everything here. And she thought that man's prime claim to superiority lay in his awareness of the flux of things, the flow and the change, a realization that raised him above the level of all other living creatures. The four of them, with Baaltje, the dog, followed the route chosen for them by their son, Edwin—the children walking on ahead, as they so much enjoyed acting as guides.

Around them the city lay in an extraordinary quiet. Turning sharply to the right at the Haarlem Gate, they found themselves in the curious world of the Western Islands. The lane by which one reached this quarter lay at so sharp an angle to the main road that one inevitably missed it and walked past. Once it was found, however, it offered them a vista over the bridges of an incredible antiquity. Here one could still come across any number of quaint old street-names, as old as the hills—the New Tar Gardens, Gallows Street, Herring Hanging. An ancient grandeur, for the most part now in a state of decay. A few, thinly scattered inhabitants. The last vestiges of a picturesque but now extinct network of streets. This was the emptiness of the museum. The waterways, the only thing really alive here, seemed a maze, though dug according to a deliberate plan. Bare wharves, with a solitary barge, washed up and stranded on the quay. Heavy lines of warehouses, some dull, some gleaming black or brown, standing shoulder to shoulder along the old fortification wall, pitted with embrasures, and between them, barren wastes or crumbling ruins, ruins left behind by the fierce fires that had raged here. Seen from bridges at the end of canals, some of the warehouses seemed to be quite inaccessible —yet paths led there all the same.

Van Marle simply revelled in it all.'   Bloesemtak
                                        (Translated by James Brockway)

As you will have noticed from this excerpt from Bordewijk and from the poet, Bloem's, sonnet, 'Dapper Street', a very different note has crept into modern writing about Amsterdam. Gone is the rhetorical praise of the city's grandeur and marvels we encountered in the poems by Vondel and

Huygens, its place having been taken by a quieter, more sober appreciation of the city's attractions. The atmosphere is conveyed, the psychological reaction to the city's being. It is not only the city and its buildings and streets that engage the modern writer's attention, but the life of its inhabitants as well. We feel this very strongly in the poem Eduard Hoornik wrote about Amsterdam just before World War II. Hoornik, a well-known poet and playwright, born in 1910, employs something of the technique of the documentary film in this poem, creating a highly moving impression in a series of shots.

AMSTERDAM

Blinds and curtains drawn and still
a ring of mist around the sun
but look, already the northern streets,
the Central Station's gleaming slates,
(and flowers along a windowsill)
have stirred and let the daylight in.

The sky swings open like a fan
clouds glimmer in the harbour pool,
a youth, crept early out of bed,
is walking past the Seamen's School;
he smells the odour of eastern spices,
he savours the names of tropic places.

And now the canals are mirrors too,
where, fleet, the young girl hurries on,
her thoughts led by the carillon,
until her footsteps reach the square,
where, by the church, he is waiting there:
young love's excitement each day new.

Beyond the canal, where slumtown lies,
a child stands by a splintered glass
and hardly dare look up, because
the night was dark with blows and cries;

it smells the odour of beer and ash,
it sees its mother ironing the wash.

From the western quarters civil servants
glide in down the rails of safe careers;
a woman stands, in her daydream staring
—how swiftly the springtime disappears—
she looks across at the faded portrait:
for him she'd abandoned all hopes, all fears.

Over Amsterdam East the day breaks too;
the dustbins stand along the streets,
somewhere a man still sits with his books,
his light has burned the whole night through...
A cheerless wall, a signboard speaks:
'Those for assistance, form a queue'.

Amsterdam South, resplendent in light,
awakens, a town of glass and steel;
a statue stands where avenues cross
alone and blind in the shining grass.
At a pane a child's hand waves until
father has disappeared from sight.

Who would know this city, heart and soul,
let him now begin, let him look and listen,
the fish has swum to the bait and bitten,
the river is tracing his silver trail,
over the port smoke spirals curl,
the lazy smoke of the wide world's shipping.

Canals and quays still dream and doze
in her heart, where the organ grinders play;
but at 'Change the prices rocket and fall...
'the world can offer, the world will pay...'
who looks down now on Damrak knows
himself the loneliest of all.   Amsterdam

(Translated by James Brockway)

REMBRANDT

Few artists enjoy a reputation as great as that of Rembrandt and few paintings enjoy the same fame as his masterpiece, The Night Watch. Born in Leyden in 1616, Rembrandt lived in Amsterdam from about his twentieth year onward. He travelled little during his life, the longest journey he ever made being very probably that to the town of Leeuwarden, in the northern province of Friesland; and he only made that because his first wife, Saskia, came from those parts.

How versatile a genius he was is apparent from the fact that, besides being a painter, he was an excellent draughtsman and unsurpassed as an etcher. What is more: he produced a great number of paintings, drawings and etchings in all sorts of different genres. His portraits are in the grand manner yet, at the same time, endowed with a penetrating insight into the heart and soul of man. And nowhere did this insight go deeper than when he was contemplating his own soul. His series of self-portraits forms a complete autobiographical study in itself, ranging from the dashing pride and elegance of the early portraits to the sober, sombre and gripping settling of accounts with human vanity which is evident in the portraits he painted of himself as an old man. Simon Vestdijk, the Dutch poet and novelist, born in 1898, writes of one of these last self-portraits in the following sonnet.

SELF-PORTRAIT

Beware of this grimace: this is no more
The gaze we knew, the immortal touch has gone.
This is the laugh of scorn we humans wear,
When, after the last defeat, life stumbles on.

No more the blossoming by which the men
Of the Golden Pleasure Garden set such store.
No more the frolics in the summer sun,
The lovely girls, themselves destined to flower.

Triumph of toothless jaws: the greybeards bite
More fiercely than the teeth of upstart youth;
They bite with their wrinkles, deep with their eyes they bite,

Eyes that, remote, from afar, reproach the young
For having flown away with the winds of Spring,
And laugh no more at life's Satanic joke.

Zelfportret
(Translated by James Brockway)

The eighteenth century, with its rigid classicism, did not accept Rembrandt's romantic and dramatic spirit, and it is only since the 19th century that he has found full recognition once more, thanks, in large measure, to Busken Huet. Huet was a writer and social historian of high calibre. His study of Dutch history in the 17th century, which was published around the year 1880, is the first book in which Holland's art, science, literature, religion as well as politics were seen as the sum total of the country's newly gained national unity. The title of the book symbolizes this unity in political and cultural life. It is called 'The Land of Rembrandt'. Here is a passage from that book:

'Anthony Leeuwenhoek, the microscope man, believed that he had been endowed by nature with eyes of a special kind so that things which appeared small to others appeared large to him.

Rembrandt was endowed with a similar gift. We can see from his etchings and drawings how sharply, how flawlessly objects were recorded on the retina of his eyes and also what extraordinary imaginative powers were his.

He had mastered the anatomy of the lion, an animal alien to his everyday environment. Various lions depicted by him, in red chalk and watercolours, can still be found in the portfolios of the connoisseurs. Some of his famous etchings depict lion hunts in a manner so true to life that one feels he must have been present at them himself. Should an elephant happen to be on show at the Amsterdam fair, the animal appears, ponderously alive, on a sheet of paper. A single impression of the artist's is sufficient to convey the sum total of the impressions of any number of visitors to the fair. He saw everything the others saw—and a great deal more besides that had escaped their notice. His depiction of the Western Church in Amsterdam is more alive, more palpable, than the image its architect, Hendrik de Keyser, can ever have had of it himself. Its tower seems to be a thing of nature.

56

Limited academic and literary knowledge could do nothing to impair the wisdom of his mind. It is evident from his allegory of the Peace of Munster that the political events of his day had significance for him. In his painting *The Concord of the State,* he treated the same subject, at the same time, as the poet Vondel did in one of his poems—and with the same originality. But he does not commit the error of reducing the Eighty Years' War to a quarrel between farmers over a drowned sheep or a cockerel with a broken leg. He finds room for a lion, a figure of Justice, hosts of horsemen, a bundle of arrows, and a coat of arms, and a reminder of the famous Beggars of 1566.

Other painters of the time are not capable of making anything more than a more or less dignified group, when painting the members of some corporation or other—a group in which the one half seems to be busy complimenting the other half, or with the whole company united around a table, tankards on their knees. They are excellent prose writers, but do not rise above the level of prose.

Rembrandt's paintings of groups, like *The Anatomy Lesson* and *The Departure for the Shooting Range* now known as the 'Night Watch', are poems. Even Frans Hals' celebrated group *The Board of the Almshouse* lacks the inimitable touch we notice in Rembrandt's painting of *The Syndics of the Cloth Guild.* He saw ordinary folk and ordinary things in an *extra*ordinary way. His art consists in the perpetual application of a process of idealization. Whether you give him his wife, Saskia, to paint, a professor of surgery, an officer of the Civic Guard, a Rabbi in his study, it does not matter—he makes ethereal creatures of them all.

He loved his profession more than he loved women, gaming and wine. And in it he discovered his true self. Despite greying whiskers and hair, in his self-portrait of the year 1660 he is still robust in appearance. Younger artists may now and then have adopted some of his idiosyncrasies, but he himself goes on searching for new colours and a new kind of luminous shadow. The experts may divide his work into different periods, yet all his periods bear witness to the same power. Death alone was capable of preventing him going on producing indefinitely. It is pointless to argue about the limitations of his talent. That he painted no ideal Madonna types like Raphael's, no Herculean male nudes like Michelangelo's and Rubens', and did not turn out the same number of elegant portraits of women as Van Dyck—everyone will admit the truth of these assertions. Yet no one would wish to be without his Susannas and his Bathshebas. What the beauty of his women lacks in nobility of contour or tenderness of expression is made up for by other qualities. It is obvious that he was not interested in depicting a seductive body, but rather in applying his light and his browns to new surfaces. He inspires such confidence in us that even when we cannot follow him, we remain convinced of his good right to do what he does. If it ought to have been done otherwise, we feel, he would have done it otherwise—for nothing was beyond his reach.'   Het land van Rembrand

(Translated by James Brockway)

Since the days of Busken Huet, Rembrandt's fame has increased enormously. Special exhibitions of his work have attracted thousands of visitors to Holland. Countless studies and biographies of him have been published, and he has also been a source of inspiration to many poets, who have felt the urge to put the emotions they experienced on contemplating his works into words. Here are the opening and closing lines of such a poem, written by Jan Engelman, born in 1900. The poem was inspired by one of Rembrandt's finest portraits, that of his son, Titus, who died at the early age of 26, in the year 1668.

TITUS READING

One morning, pale the light, he came upon
His son (so dear to him, he could dispel
All thoughts of other things) —he found him there,
Seated before him, believing himself unseen,
Reading—with a laugh about his mouth,
Eyes riveted, the eyebrows slightly raised,
And gently parted lips—reading some work of wit.
Oh, see the graceful cadence of his locks,
Like some noblewoman's, all golden rings and curls.
His cap is not set on his head, it soars,
Half deep in the neck, half halo in the air.
He smiles, who close now to the bitter grave,
Sits dreaming here of life's rich plenitude ...
... his eyelids seem

Like doves in the nest, his hands too delicate;
This is no child who'll stay long at his side—
And Rembrandt feels a sudden surge of power,
His brush sweeps over the rough face of the wood.
As though he had never, in all those days and nights,
Cursed heavy fate, the fear that cleaved his heart,
On seeing this fragility, on catching Death's cruel nod.
Now he must give the dearest he can give:
The flesh becomes spirit, the paint paternal love.   Lezende Titus
                                        (Translated by James Brockway)

And here, finally, are two verses from a poem written by Garmt Stuiveling, a poem inspired by the contemplation of Rembrandt's portrait of his young wife, Saskia, which hangs in the museum at Kassel, Germany.

Little princess, in silks arrayed,
In crimson velvet, gold brocade,
So shy, so diffident, you seem
Like one caught in a waking dream—
Half disbelieving, half in dread . . .
The ostrich feather on your head,
The clustered pearls, the amethysts,
The bangles on your slender wrists,
These royal robes and jewels you wear
Are yours yet have an alien air,
For though it gives, life takes away,
Sparing nor youth nor rich array.

> .   .   .   .

Little princess in silks arrayed,
You turn your full-lit face aside,
Struck, so it seems, by something near—
Perhaps it was some gaudy flower,
A voice, a footstep, or a light
Beyond the daylight, and so bright,
So strange, you wait with bated breath,
With parted lips—until you laugh

Aside the sudden pang of fear
With which Death makes even you aware,
You, whom no loss has yet dismayed,
Little princess, in silks arrayed.

Bij Rembrandt's portret van Saskia
(Translated by James Brockway)

THE SEA

The sea is Holland's traditional enemy. The poet Marsman ended his 'Home Thoughts from Abroad' poem with the lines:

And far and wide
the voice of the water,
of endless disaster,
is feared and heard.

In the Middle Ages most Dutchmen built their towns and villages well inland, far from the sea's threatening roar. For them the broad beaches and white dunes of the Dutch coastline had nothing of the attraction they have for the Dutchman of modern times.

With the Age of Discovery, however, the sea acquired a new significance. It was now no longer simply an enemy, battering at the dykes, but the highroad to new worlds of adventure, and to the fabulous riches of the East. Dutch merchant seamen now began to build up a great empire in the East Indies. Shipping was the source of Amsterdam's wealth and greatness and it provides the key and answer to that remarkable phenomenon, the 17th century period of sudden economic and cultural flowering we know as the Golden Age of the Netherlands, the age of Rembrandt, Vermeer, and of the Dutch national poet Vondel. Vondel, in fact, wrote a grand poem in praise of the mercantile marine in which he recounts all the blessings that her shipping had bestowed upon the country.

We have to wait until more recent times, however, before writers and poets begin to describe the individual's reaction to the sea and the moods it evokes in him. Modern man's response to nature is entirely the product of the Romantic Movement. In Holland it dates from the mid-18th century, when the flight from urban civilization caused men to turn to the countryside, to the woods, the heaths, the moon, stars and sea, in search of solitude and communion with nature. For a time poems of the sea continue to catalogue all the details of sea battles lost and won, and it is only with the arrival of Impressionism that poetry throws this ballast overboard and we find the poet standing alone, confronted by the sea, and writing of his personal response to that experience. In Holland a literary revolution took place in the eighteen-eighties, a revolution which brought to the fore a new school of poets known as the *Tachtigers*, that is, the Men of the Eighties. Here is a famous poem by one of the leading poets of that movement, Willem Kloos, who lived from 1859 to 1938.

The note he strikes has now become completely outmoded, but in his own day it was entirely new to Dutch literature.

> *The Sea, the Sea pounds on in endless wild commotion,*
> *The Sea in which my Soul itself reflected sees.*
> *The Sea is like my Soul, for, like my Soul, the Ocean,*
> *A Thing of Living Beauty, to itself a stranger is.*
>
> *It laves its waters clear in eternal, pure ablutions,*
> *And never it fails to turn and flow back whence it flees;*
> *Expressing itself in waves, whorls, eddies, convolutions,*
> *Singing its ever-joyous, its ever-mournful lays.*
>
> *O Sea, were I like Thee, of myself as unaware,*
> *Then, and only then, would true happiness be mine.*
> *Then, only then, were I free from longing and despair*
> *From the hunger for joy and pain for which the heart doth pine.*
> *Then my Soul were indeed a Sea, and its freedom from all care,*
> *Since greater It is than Thee, would greater be than Thine.*
>
> (Translated by James Brockway)

After Kloos, with his passionate approach and his high-flown language, the following brief poem by A. Roland Holst, one of the most celebrated figures among the older generation of contemporary Dutch poets, forms a striking contrast. Born in 1888, Roland Holst was in his youth strongly influenced by the early poetry of W. B. Yeats, and much of his work is heavily charged with the melancholy atmosphere of 'Celtic twilight' and of glory past and done. The sea, which in one line he has called an 'inhuman wilderness', occurs time and again in his poems as a sombre and compelling image of the infinite and timeless and of a world existing

62

beyond the boundaries of human experience. In the following poem, however, he strikes a rather different note.

THE LITTLE POOL

Sometimes I half imagine that the sea,
Since powerful it seems, my whole life long will be
The tempestuous reality,
With which I can withstand the world,
Come good, come ill.
But that, in the end, I will
Probe to death's secret beside the little pool
That held the storm-racked evening sky
so quietly reflected in its eye.
De kleine waterplek
(Translated by James Brockway)

At the turn of the century the sea provided the theme of a Dutch stage play which became well-known outside Holland as well. Written by the playwright, Herman Heyermans, and entitled 'The Good Hope', it portrayed the hardships endured by the fishing community in Holland at the time, and thanks to its dramatic structure, it still drew full houses long after the abuses it castigates had been brought to an end. Dutch authors of today have not forgotten that the sea links their country with distant and exotic continents. Many of them have sailed the Seven Seas and written about their experiences.

The following two prose extracts present a sharp contrast between the quiet, deserted waters of a tiny port on the Zuyder Zee in Holland, and the tumultuous, crowded scene of a ship, laden with human cargo, arriving off the coast of China. The first comes from an early short story, called 'The Brown Friend', by a leading Dutch novelist of recent times, Simon Vestdijk.

'A cool, west wind, a more humid atmosphere, the distant wink of the elegant tower of the lighthouse, these announced the sea. I now suddenly caught sight of him far to the left, heading for the small harbour which, embraced by two short piers, hardly had a right to the name, so silted up as it was. Fishing boats could never get more than halfway in, the other half being navigable only for rowing boats, and they, too, usually lay tied up, the joint property of the local community, especially of the children.

If you were a sprouting lad, all you needed to do was to strike up a friendship with some idle loafer of a fisherman and you were soon the master of one of these boats. The grammar school boys in any case never had to pay for using them, and there was even no charge for damage inflicted.

As I followed Hugo across the stretch of sand that came out at the North Pier, seeing him stumble now and then over lumps of wood and loose strands of barbed wire, I still had no idea of what he was going to do. The moon was shining so bright that my eye could discern lines of silvery blue stretching from just outside the harbour's mouth almost to the horizon. There, everything was enveloped in a distant, thin mist, forced skywards by the moon, pressed down again by the wind—or perhaps it rose up spontaneously out of the weird rising and ebbing water that encircled the Grint Flats, lying out at sea, half an hour's rowing away, and submerged at high tide.

Although I'd been there often enough, this sandbank now took on a far more mysterious meaning for me than before, simply because the sea seemed to stretch so surprisingly far and bare in that direction now, even though it was not directly lit like the sparkling waters of the harbour, along which I could see Hugo limping figure moving. But it was not until he began to descend one of the flights of steps roughly hewn out of the basalt that I realized that he, too, must be feeling the strange attraction exerted by that mysterious, fluctuating island, far out at sea. Perhaps he longed to be out there, in the cool, open wastes of the sea, to feel the spray splashing against his cheeks, after the company he had just left. I concealed myself behind a plump mooring pile, painted black and white and smelling of tar, and waited to see what he was going to do. It was a strange sight, that limping figure stepping into one of the little rowing boats, placing one of the oars into the rowlocks and pushing off with the other. The ripples in the water spread out to the two piers. In the deserted harbour there was no other sound but the splash of his oars.'

De bruine vriend   (Translated by James Brockway)

And here, in contrast to that quiet scene set in the Zuyder Zee, is the opening of the novel 'Life on Earth' by J. Slauerhoff, a young poet and novelist of the pre-war period whose premature death, in 1936, robbed

Drawing by Vincent van Gogh

Saskia van Uylenburg by Rembrandt (Museum Kassel, Germany)

Dutch literature of one of its most virile talents. For years a ship's doctor, Slauerhoff knew the sea, ships and seamen like no other Dutch author, as a sailor, and as a poet visionary. Here is how his novel begins:

'An old summer's day off the China coast, which for centuries has permitted the quiet waters of the Southern Sea to wash over and scoop out its grey rocks and cliffs, its brown shores, without having yielded one inch.

There is practically no movement to be seen but for a gentle swell, the water eddying around rocky promontories, fleets of fishing boats passing in quiet swarms along the coast, solitary junks, laden with cargo, gliding slowly from harbour to harbour, as though lost in meditation. The European's steamships chug hastily in and out, but go almost unnoticed. Everything still remains the same.

An old summer's day, the same as many before it: a ship approaches the islands on which Amoy has raised its walls. It is an ancient steamer, painted black and on the small side. Yet it is bringing fifteen hundred souls back to their native land. The wealthy from Singapore, merchants from Malaya, from every island in the Indies, returning after years of absence with a small capital and a large family of wives, sons and daughters; coolies, who sold themselves for three years and were kept for five in poisonous tin mines and on scorching rubber plantations, and who are now coming back home, with flabby muscles and caved in cheeks—but with a belt fat with money, with silver dollars, round their waists.

All these are housed together, on top of and underneath and mixed up with one another, down in the holds and up on the sizzling steel plates of the deck, wherever there is room for them among the pinnaces, cranes and cargo. They include the newly born, as soft and smooth as small molluscs, whose great brown eyes lie so open and so vulnerable in their tiny faces. And there are the very old, whose loose skin sags down, like too voluminous a robe, around their mellow bones, and who are coming back to die in the Land of Lands. Some of them die on board; there are as many coffins as there are pinnaces on the after deck. They lie on a layer of quicklime, the coffin lid against their faces. But they will arrive at their destination all the same. Merchants swing fat, protruding paunches proudly before them—the physical symbol of their wealth. Opium smokers sit in corners like bundles of dry tinder, deaf and blind to their surroundings.

But all of them, children, greybeards, the sick, the corpses, the human wrecks and the paunches, all form a whole, a chunk of humanity, that is going to China. A hum and buzz, as of some gigantic insect, emanates from the lower deck, an odour steams up from them all and hangs heavily about the ship.

Amoy is now in sight... The ship drops anchor far from the town under a sheet of rain. But in hardly no time the boats start to arrive from the lodging houses. Twenty, thirty large sampans cluster about the ship. The touts throw up ropes and swarm with slimy feet up its sides. At the same time squibs are let off, exploding erratically, all over the place.

Gone now is the silence of the sea, the monotonous hum. Shrill cries pierce the air. The touts grasp hold of people and tug them along with them, dragging away their luggage and dropping it into their boats. How will the owners ever be able to trace it again in the turmoil and confusion? The new arrivals are annoyed, but it is not for long. Everyone accepts his fate—and his place in his boat. They move in an unending stream down the ladders. Tiny children are carried in loin-cloths, old women on the back. Their tight, combed hair, their black jackets gleam in the rain; their stumps of teeth grin shorewards...'

Het leven op aarde
(Translated by James Brockway)

66

THE FARMER

The contrast between townsman and countryman is a theme which can be traced very early on in Dutch and Flemish literature.

The townsman had two very different conceptions of his country brother. Sometimes he looks upon him as a stupid and ludicrous bumpkin, who consequently got the comic rôles handed out to him in the early farces and comedies. On the other hand, the refined and decadent townsman often showed a tendency to take the countryman, and especially the shepherd, as a symbol of virtue and unspoiled simplicity. The pastoral poems and plays which embodied this idea originated in Italy.

In medieval times, however, Dutch and Flemish towns were small and the life lived in them relatively simple and modest, so there was no real call for pastoral plays and poems to point out the virtues of the rustic life. In fact, the nobility and townsfolk of those days took a far more realistic view of the peasant, seeing him as rough and brutish, and also as a threat to their way of life. This is forcibly illustrated in the following verses, quoted from an anonymous Flemish ballad.

THE SONG OF THE CHURLS

Let us sing of the Churls. Their hordes
Would make the devil afeared.
They would subdue the lords.
They wear an unkempt beard.
Their ragged clothes are fit for a sty.
Their hats too small for their heads.
Their hoods are all awry.
Their hose and shoes are worn to shreds.
With bread and cheese and curd and gruel
All day they stuff their guts.
It makes the churl a fool:
He never eats but gluts.

To the kermis goes the lout.
Then he thinks himself a duke.
And there he lays about

With a rusty stave or crook.
He starts to drink of the wine,
And in his drunken drawl
He sings, 'The world is mine,
City, land and all.'
With bread and cheese and curd and gruel
All day they stuff their guts.
It makes the churl a fool:
He never eats but gluts.

Then he will treat the boys
To the bagpipe's tirrelirit.
Lord, what a hellish noise,
For decent ears unfit.
They jump to their feet and dance.
Their long beards bounce as well,
They stamp and run and prance.
God send them all to hell.
With bread and cheese and curd and gruel
All day they stuff their guts.
It makes the churl a fool:
He never eats but gluts.

Het kerelslied

(Translated by Adriaan J. Barnouw)

For centuries art remained confined to the town. That is why a certain Hubert Corneliszoon Poot became so famous in the early 18th century. Poot was both a farmer and a poet, and people came from towns far and wide to see this unusual phenomenon. His great poem 'Akkerleven'—'The Farmer's Life'—which he wrote in praise of the country life, was obviously based on the work of the Latin poet, Horace, notably on his 'Beatus ille' Here we get a very different picture of the peasant and his life than the one drawn for us in 'The Song of the Churls'. To the 18th century Dutchman, the farmer's life had become idyllic, his lot sweeter by far than that of the poor townsman, buried among bricks and mortar. Or, at least, this is what Poot tells the lawyer, Cornelis 'sGravenzande, to whom he had dedicated his poem, some verses of which follow:

THE FARMER'S LIFE

How pleasant is the lot
Of simple Country John,
Who with king nor any man
Would exchange his lowly cot.
Sweet content's of richer worth
Than all the pomp and show on earth!

When our John his oxen sees,
As behind his plough they toil
Through his own, ancestral soil,
'Neath the shade of lofty trees,
Or his wheatfield doth behold,
How it crowns the clods with gold,

Or his smooth milch cows doth hear,
Ever healthy, ever hale,
Lowing in some winding vale—
The which is music to his ear—
City, poor for all your pleasures,
Show me such delights and treasures!

Fertile acres, woody nooks,
Lush, green meadows, beasts at play,
Fresh farm butter, curds and whey,
Crystal springs and limpid brooks,
Rich abundance, full, replete,
Makes our country living sweet.

Plucking apples from the boughs,
Mowing, reaping grasses tall,
Filling barn and shed and stall,
Shearing sheep and milking cows,
Seven children and a wife
His delight and joy in life.

Tell me, learned sGravenzand',
You who know now from my rhyme
How our farmer spends his time,
Tell me, Lawyer of the Land,
Since my song's inscribed to you,
Who lives sweeter, tell me who?

Akkerleven
(Translated by James Brockway)

Since the mid 19th century the country has once again become a favourite subject for our authors. In the beginning these authors were townsmen who romanticized rural life and consequently painted a false picture of it. Here, too, Impressionism was a wholesome influence. Perhaps no writer in Dutch has given us a more impressive picture of the true life of the farmer than the Flemish novelist Stijn Streuvels, who was born in 1871. In his novel, 'De Vlaschaard' (The Flax Field), Streuvels depicts the tragedy of the conflict between two generations of farmers, of the struggle between conservatism and progress. Here are two extracts from this novel. The first is the portrait of the father, the second that of his son.

'He sat there, the full weight of his broad body filling the chair, his heavy head bent forward, his knees drawn up and his arms resting in his lap, puffing away at his ancient, crusted pipe. The flames twisted up out of the wood chips at his feet. He was aware of himself, sitting there: he knew full well that he represented unity on this great farm, that he was the controller of all its teeming activity, with the laws and the ordering of the entire farming year, and the plans for many another, in his head. It stretched out like a smooth, broad road in his mind, everything he had to do—and in his firm grip he held both means and results, safe and secure. He kept the same firm grasp on all the smaller, everyday details, too, as he did on the main plans for the future. He knew the exact condition of everything that lived and moved on his farm, even to the remotest corner of farmyard, barn and stable. He knew every farmhand, youth or maid, as well as he knew his own children; and he was the first one to notice if anything was wrong with any animal in his stables and stalls or in any of the meadows. Even if it were merely the case of some harness support that was about to snap, or some screw or other that had worked loose, he saw it. He was aware that it was his will alone that kept all this movement and activity going, and that everything pursued the course he himself had laid down for it with his own, powerful will.

It was winter outside and cold and poverty reigned in the region all around. But the roof of his farm provided a sure shelter for all his underlings, and everyone who lent a hand with the work on the farm was safe from want and the wet. Here everyone could feed himself fat the whole winter through. Everyone willing to labour in the summertime, he thought, shall find a warm nest to creep into here in the winter. He knew how his own weighty presence inspired awe in others, reducing men to silence everywhere he went. He had inherited this sway over others from his father and he had maintained his authority by dint of a stubborn will . . . and by hard work. He ruled his farm like a king and enjoyed the reputation throughout the district of being as firm as a rock, mightier than any other farmer for miles around. Surly and gruff of manner, he it was who gave the other farmers advice; he who had the say among them, he who kept the old traditions alive, he who farmed his land according to time-honoured custom, he for whom the others would wait before starting to sow, to harvest, or to embark on any of the other manifold operations of farming. 'Vermeulen is doing it', 'Vermeulen isn't doing it', these words had the authority of an order that was obeyed and respected throughout the region.'

And now, the son:

'Louis was the stalwart young farmer, the fine fellow with a powerful body and a sturdy pair of legs in his boots. The fellow with the ruddy cheeks and the wideawake eyes, who, oblivious to bad weather, went cheerfully on his way, a stranger to boredom and anger. He was in the full flush of his twenties, the young farmer moving freely about his father's land like a stallion in its prime that is unaware of any limitations to its strength and exuberance, at home with everything that was going on the farm—for he had been born and bred on it, had grown up as part of it. He was the new driving force, the new voice, the power ascendant, who gave full rein to his abundant vigour and went his own way on the great holding, side by side with the old farmer, the high chief, authority and dominion personified, that his father was.'

(Translated by James Brockway)

These extracts from Stijn Streuvels' novel provide an illustration of the regional novel. From around the year 1890 onward numerous Flemish and Dutch writers have followed Streuvels's example and almost every region has its own story-tellers who have written novels devoted to country-life, and so made their contribution to Dutch literature.

To conclude with here is a well-known ballad by J. W. F. Werumeus Buning, 1891-1958, one which has acquired great popularity in Holland, showing as it does, the fundamental continuity and sameness of the farmer's work throughout the turmoil of world history.

THE BALLAD OF THE FARMER

Three crosses stood on Golgotha,
But the farmer, he stuck to his plough.
Magdalene, Mary, Veronica,
But the farmer he stuck to his plough.
And when he had finished ploughing his field,
The farmer turned round his plough,
And down beside it the farmer kneeled,
And God listened to his vow.

O, many a man had a wondrous dream,
But the farmer, he stuck to his plough.
Thermopylae, Salamis and Troy,
But the farmer, he stuck to his plough.
And every year the corn grows green,
The stars shine bright in the sky,
And into the world God sent the Word,
But the farmer, he stuck to his plough.

They have burnt down his farm and murdered his wife,
They have slaughtered his ox and his cow,
Then he girded the harness about his own loins,

And the farmer, he stuck to his plough.
Napoleon crossed the snowy Alps
And saw him at work in his field,
He sailed from St. Helena, proud on the prow,
But the farmer, he stuck to his plough.

And better than he there is many a man
Who has heard of the world and its woe,
Who has turned aside at the sight of wrong
And surrendered him to the foe.
Many a man turned the plough on its side
And abandoned his work and his vow,
But the lark, he continued to sing the same song,
And the farmer, he stuck to his plough.

Lord God, in the grass the farmer lay
And the farmer he dreamt this dream:
That at last there had come a holiday
As St. John had promised him.
And there, to his left, the wicked passed,
To his right the good did bow,
But never his name did he hear on the list,
And the farmer, he stuck to his plough.

But when he saw the heavens aglow,
Ablaze with a radiant light,
He unharnessed then his horse from the plough,
Wiped off the sweat from his toilworn brow,
Knelt down beside his silent bay
And awaited what God should say.
And the farmer, he heard a great voice break
Over earth and sky and sea:
'For the farmer who stuck to his plough, for his sake,
Let the world continue to be!'

Ballade van den boer
(Translated by James Brockway)

FREEDOM

Lying surrounded by countries which have known centuries of highly centralized and despotic government, Holland has always been a country remarkable for its religious and political tolerance and for the large measure of individual freedom enjoyed by its citizens. In the 16th and 17th centuries the struggle for national freedom against Spain gave rise to a great number of patriotic songs which were mainly written to existing melodies. The fight for political freedom went hand in hand with the Reformation and so many of these songs had a strong religious undertone. A famous song included in the memorial songbook compiled by Valerius is 'O Nederland, let op Uw Saeck', in which the Prince of Orange calls on his countrymen to defend their hard-won freedom against Spanish trickery. Here is a translation of the first verse:

Oh Holland take heed, guard well your cause,
The time, the hour, is near.
Lest you lose the freedom which is yours
The which I do aver
Your fathers have so dearby bought
To make it yours for aye.
That costly prize they have not sought
For you to yield away.

(Translated by James Brockway)

It was not until the 19th century that social freedom began in the Netherlands. The second half of that century was characterized by two freedom movements: the emancipation of women and the emancipation of the working classes. In these movements—and in many others as well—it was Eduard Douwes Dekker, writing under the name of Multatuli, who publicized these new ideas in a brilliant way. In 1860, idealism and sarcasm gave us that masterpiece entitled 'Max Havelaar', a book which turned the way in which the colonies were run into a moral issue. After that Multatuli proceeded to attack every form of authority, in the church, the state, in society, in art and in the family. Once he had published the story of

Thugatèr in 1861, the emancipation of women soon developed into a movement and, half a century later, it became a fact.

Here is the story of Thugatèr.

Thugatèr milked her father's cows and she milked them well, for the milk she brought home yielded more butter than the milk brought home by her brothers. I will tell you why this was. He who milks patiently, to the very last drop, comes home with milk rich in cream, but he who hurries through his task, leaves the cream behind. And Thugatèr, you see, was not in a hurry. But her brothers were. For they claimed they had a right to know something more, besides milking their father's cows. But *she* knew nothing about rights.

'My father has taught me to shoot with the bow and arrow,' said one of the brothers. 'I can live by hunting, and I want to roam the earth and work on my own account.'

'Me he taught to fish,' said the second brother. 'I'd be foolish to do nothing else but milk for someone else.'

'He showed me how to build a boat,' cried the third. 'I'm going to fell a tree and sit in it on the water. I want to know what there is to see on the other side of the lake.'

'I want to go and live with fair-haired Gunè,' said a fourth, 'and have a home of my own, with daughters like Thugatèr to milk for me.'

Thus each one of the brothers had a wish, a desire, a will.

And they were so preoccupied with their desires that they had no time to take the cream, which the cows, highly disconsolate, were obliged to retain, of no use to anyone at all. But Thugatèr milked to the very last drop.

'Father,' cried the brothers, 'we're leaving you!'

'Who will milk the cows?' asked the father.

'Why, Thugatèr, of course!'

'And what will happen, if she, too, feels the urge to go sailing, fishing, hunting and to see the world? What will happen, if she, too, thinks of going to live with someone, dark or fair, so as to have a home of her own and all that goes with it? I can do without you, but I can't do without her ... for the milk she brings home is rich and full of cream.'

Then, after conferring together, the sons said:

'Father, *you must teach her nothing,* and she'll then go on milking to the end of her days. Do not show her how a strung cord pulled tight and released can shoot an arrow into the air—and she will not want to go out hunting. Conceal from her the ways of the fish, which will swallow a sharp hook if it is covered with bait—and she will not think of casting out lines and nets. Do not teach her how to hollow out a tree and how you can then sail away in it to the other side of the lake—and she will then feel no longing to see the other side. And never let her know she can obtain a home of her own and all that goes with is, with a dark one or a fair one! Never let her know these things, oh father, and she will remain with you and you will get rich, creamy milk from your cows! But allow us to depart, father, each one according to his desire!'

Thus spoke the sons.

But the father, who was a very cautious man, resumed:

'Prithee, who shall prevent her from learning what I have not taught her myself? What will happen, if she spies the bluebottle sailing on a floating twig? What if the taut thread of her wool snaps back of its own accord and happens to drive the shuttle across her loom? What if at the brook's edge she sees the fish as it bites at the wriggling worm, misses its aim in its eagerness, and gets caught on the sharp sheath of the reeds? And what, finally, if she discovers the little nest the larks build in the clover in the month of May?'

The sons then conferred together once again and said:

'She will not learn anything from these things, father. She is too stupid to make the step from knowledge to desire. We, too, should never have known anything, if you had not taught us yourself.'

But the father replied:

'No, she is not stupid. I fear that she will learn by herself, things which you needed me to teach you. Thugatèr is not stupid.'

Then the sons considered the matter again—this time more deeply— and said:

'Tell her, father, that *to know, to understand* and *to desire* are *sinful* in a girl!' This time the highly cautious father was satisfied. He allowed his sons to depart, to fish, to hunt, to wed, anywhere they might choose. But for Thugatèr knowledge, understanding and desire were proscribed, and she went on milking, in ignorance, to the very end.

And so things have remained to this day. Minnebrieven

(Translated by James Brockway)

The working class struggle was the second great movement for emancipation. Socialism has had a very marked influence on Dutch writing, Henriëtte Roland Holst, one of the greatest poets of the early decades of this century, was a convinced and militant socialist and showed it in her work. Her poetry is marked by its strong ethical feeling, and by feelings, too, of guilt and forgiveness.

In May 1940, our nation's freedom, which but for a short period during the Napoleonic era had been taken for granted since 1648, was suddenly violated by the invading armies of Nazi Germany. In the end, the attack on democracy, on spiritual traditions, on security and on life itself, failed. But not before tens of thousands of innocent people had been carried off and murdered. The world-famous 'Diary of Anne Frank' conveys an impression of the suffering of the Dutch Jews. The Dutch Resistance found a voice in poetry printed secretly, to which scores of writers contributed anonymously. Of this there is no more vivid example than the following poem by Jan Campert, who, though not one of these eighteen, met his death in a German concentration camp.

THE SONG OF THE EIGHTEEN WHO DIED

My cell is only two yards long
And barely six foot wide;
But smaller still will be the place
Where soon I shall abide;
Nameless shall I be resting there
Together with my pals;
Of eighteen of us none will be
Alive when ev'ning falls.

Oh loveliness of sky and land,
Of Holland's field and dune!
Once subjugated by the foe
I could not rest—but soon
I thought, what can a faithful soul
In times like these begin?
He can but kiss his wife and child
And fight—to lose or win.

I knew the task that I began,
Its call to dangerous work,
But he whose heart is pledged to it
No danger shall he shirk;
He knows how freedom in this land
Was honoured above all,
'Ere an accursed alien hand
Gave out a different call.

'Ere he, who swears but breaks his oath
Accomplished his foul job,
Invading Holland's peaceful soil
To kill, and burn and rob;
'Ere he, who claims that honour is
German monopoly,
His heel set on our people's neck
And stole what he could see.

The Pied Piper of Berlin
Now pipes his melody;
But sure as I shall soon be dead,
No more my love shall see
Nor ever more break bread with her
Or share her couch again,
Reject all that he offers you,
It bears his bloody stain!

Remember, you who read these lines
My comrades' agony,
And first of all, those left behind:
Comforted they must be;
We, too, thought of our people and
The land where we were born.
Assuredly this cloud will pass
As night before the dawn.

Now through my tiny window creeps
A timid morning ray;
Oh, Heav'n make my departure light,
And if I've failed, I pray
(As ev'ryone indeed may fail)
Grant me Thy mercy, God,
That I may face death like a man
Before the firing squad.

Het lied der achttien doden
(Translated by Emile van Loo)

THE CHILD

Nowadays the child often forms the subject of serious literature, but this has not always been the case. During the Middle Ages it seems that the thoughts and feelings aroused by the child and the child-parent relationship found artistic expression exclusively via the symbol of the Virgin Mary and the Child Jesus. In the 17th century, the Golden Age in the Netherlands' history, the child was frequently portrayed by our painters, though the interest they showed in the child found little echo among the poets of the time. Interest, that is to say, in the living child—for of poems about children who had died there were plenty. Both Vondel and Poot wrote a number of highly moving verses of this nature, one of which, Vondel's 'My Daughter Departing...' has already been quoted.

It is the Romantic Movement that we have to thank for introducing the child into literature as a being existing in its own right, a small world in the process of 'becoming'. About the year 1780 two women authors, Mesdames Wolff and Deken, wrote a novel—one of the very first in Dutch literature—entitled 'Sara Burgerhart', which took a young girl as its heroine. In the same period, an aristocratic and pious poet, one Hiëronymus van Alphen (1746-1803), achieved unprecedented success with a number of volumes of verses for and about children, many of which were translated into several languages.

The first writer, however, to venture to put all the experiences of childhood into a novel was Multatuli, the famous 19th century novelist, who lived from 1820 to 1887. This book, 'Woutertje Pieterse', although never completed, is a masterpiece, a true classic. Towards the close of the 19th century, a medical student, Frederik van Eeden (1860-1932) wrote an enchanting book, entitled 'De Kleine Johannes'—Little Johan—which won deserved fame both in Holland and, in a number of translations, abroad. Van Eeden was also a poet and the following poem, in a translation by Adriaan J. Barnouw, is about one of his own children, a very young baby.

HIS FIRST SMILE

It was his first, first smile! He had flown
From a faraway and soundless zone.

80

Multatuli (Eduard Douwes Dekker) (1820-1887)

Mother and Child by Frans Hals (Museum Dahlem-Berlin)

There he had neither hearing nor sight,
And only lived by an inner light.

Solitude is there. Not a single thing
Is expected or leaves remembering.
Nothing is there but earnestness.
The night is without sadness, and laughterless.

He had in himself that void's austerity,
When he came to this loud, light pageantry,
The sounds and the faces of grown-up things,
The lights, the lamps, the glitterings.

To its strangeness he was indifferent.
He had no connection with this new event,
Until he looked at his mother and father, while
Watching the wonder in their smile.

He did not understand that baffling sign
Of lips drawn in a curving line.
That sign of love, with a faint distress
(Through knowing the past and distantness).

He thought to close within the grip
Of his comprehension, as on a ship
The helmsman, in waters new to him,
Sees through the mist a signal gleam.

He let his wondering star eyes go
From me to his mother, to and fro,
As if from his immost heart he would wring
An answer to that signalling.

Then it seemed, of a sudden, as if a bird
Deep within him woke and stirred

And started singing beautifully
Songs of gladness and memory.

Like flowers from the distant twilight world
Awareness and understanding unfurled;
He answered our signal of love with his own:
He smiled—and ceased to be alone.   Toen ons kindje glimlachte

Many of the books about children that have appeared, in large numbers, during the past half century have been autobiographical. This is especially evident in the works of the painter and author, Jacobus van Looy, who lived from 1855 to 1930, and who has described his childhood and youth—spent in an orphanage in Haarlem—in a work of three volumes. His painter's eye saw things more sharply than the normal eye—his story is full of visual imagery. Of great charm, too, are some of the autobiographical short stories of Louis Couperus, mentioned in our first talk, many of whose novels appeared in English versions. The following fragment comes from one of his short stories of the East Indies in the 1870s.

'We were in the Indies. I was a child of nine at the time and one day I went with mama to the old town, to a Chinese cabinet-maker's. He was a joiner, who was highly skilled and who carved and collected, sold and copied, antique furniture, like the furniture you sometimes see in the *campong*. His carvings were extremely beautiful. I still remember how lovely I thought they were, even though I was only a child at the time.

Well now, I went with mama to his workshop to choose some antique chairs . . . He received mama very politely, as Chinese merchants always do, with much bowing and an abundance of flattering words. But suddenly, on catching sight of me, he gave a slight start, as though struck by something unusual, whereupon he made a deep obeisance before me, not once, but three times, four times, and called his wife and sons, who all came and made deep bows in front of me, accompanied by many flattering words and gestures of the utmost respect. I shall never forget it . . . I was a child of nine, and those Chinese, all bowing to me, made a very deep impression on me . . .

Puzzled, my mother said: 'But why are you bowing to my little boy like that? Tell me, Baba. And why are your wife and your sons all bowing to him?'

And then, very humbly, the Chinese cabinet-maker said: 'Honourable lady, we are bowing to your son, the little gentleman, because he bears on his body a highly auspicious sign. Were you not aware of that, honourable lady? Look, in his hair, on his forehead, the little master has a small tuft of hair, just like the one everyone else has at the back of his head. A little tuft of hair like that at the front of the head, on the forehead, is a very rare and highly auspicious sign. The little gentleman bears the mark of great fortune. For a little tuft of hair at the front of the head signifies that one has a 'great soul'...'

'You must not make my little boy vain, Baba,' said my mother. 'And he will become vain, if you start telling him he has a 'great soul', as you say.'

And, secretly highly impressed, I was busy asking myself what it could mean, to have a 'great soul', and I searched in myself, a boy of nine, for my 'great soul'.

Then, in deep earnest, the Chinese cabinet-maker said:

'I do not mean it in that sense, honourable lady ... Perhaps I do not express myself quite clearly in the Malay language. In my own language I would say that the little tuft of hair at the front of the head marks the young gentleman as one possessing a 'great soul'. By that I mean that the young gentleman will be fortunate in the life that lies ahead of him, because his soul will be 'great', and he will look about him and will see all the beauty there is on earth and in people. The 'great souls' who have that vision are the artists and poets. They imitate nature and life, and the things they make in this way are the source of their happiness in life. Their souls are 'great', because they see many things and understand many things, and in their turn they give of what they have received, for their souls are gentle and mild. And because they receive and give and see and admire and imitate, they are happy, their lives are happier than those of most other people. They are the darlings of the Gods and the Gods love them ...'

Those were the Chinese cabinet-maker's exact words, but it was only later in life that I understood them properly. All the same, I was deeply impressed at the time, for his sons, big Chinese boys, were standing there, smiling at me and bowing and pointing at the tuft of hair on my forehead.

My mother was a simple, kindly woman. I discerned a slight frown on her face and understood that she was afraid the Chinese cabinet-maker was making too much of me on account of my little tuft of hair, just as she would sometimes frown when acquaintances or her lady friends said that I was a 'dear little boy' ...

But as she now turned the conversation into other channels by enquiring about the carved chairs, I approached the altar at the rear of the shop.

The Chinese boys clustered around me, smiling and courteous. I looked up at the great Chinese religious picture. The picture of the Gods who would bless me and love me. There were two of them. One was benignly plump, smiling, all pink and white, in a magnificent robe of gold, and with long drooping moustaches hanging down from his lips ... The other, darting about behind him, was bent and twisted, with a horrible grimace on his face, with bloodshot eyes, black and scarlet of countenance, hair and beard, and stretching out fingers with pointed, enormously long nails on them.

The Chinese boys lighted sticks of incense standing in slender vases. The smoke curled upwards to the ceiling, a pale blue.

The Black God leered at me through the smoke. The rosy, fat God smiled at me good-naturedly. Full of confidence, I gazed up at my Gods, who would 'bless me' and 'love me', because I had a little tuft of hair at the front of my head.

I thought the good-natured God nice and the black one did not scare me so very much. I thought him funny rather than frightening, with his fiery, red beard; and besides, I thought his robe, of black, gold and red, very beautiful indeed...'

(Translated by James Brockway)

And now three short poems by three modern Dutch poets, each of which deals in its different way with the relationship existing between the grown-up and the child—either his own child, or the child he was in the past.

The first is by Edgar du Perron, one of several writers of great talent whom Holland lost at the beginning of World War II.

THE CHILD WE WERE

Life we find sweetest in the past that's dead,
on the furthest edge of memory's domain—

the lie of childhood days, the promise vain
of all we were going to do, and never did.

Day of tin soldiers, prayers beside the bed,
of mother's goodnight kiss, of perfume blown,
the purest source of happiness and pain,
of wonder and of friendships never said.

His, on our walls, is the portrait we love best,
this child, deep in a lap, in broad hands held,
even now in his eye a dark, a strange mistrust.

Long-vanished self, small, solitary child,
for whom such bitter, idle tears we've shed
among the fading portraits of the Dead.

Het kind dat wij waren
(Translated by James Brockway)

Next, a poem by Eduard Hoornik whose sense of human tragedy is evident everywhere in his work. The poem delicately conveys the subtle link between the parent's life and his child's.

MY DAUGHTER AND I

While reading, I feel my daughter turn and look
at me: I go on reading, give no sign.
Her life lies on my lap, an open book,
its every page a replica of mine.

No one finds more than a trace of happiness;
there's nothing I can do to help her win
what I, having scarcely won, let slip again;
she, too, will know the hunger and the loss.

I close the book. We sit there, side by side,
yet do not speak, do not exchange a word—
simply a glance, a smile, but it is then

as though I'm staring into my own two eyes,
and what lies there as clear as water lies,
as slowly I merge into myself again.

Mijn dochter en ik
(Translated by James Brockway)

Finally, a poem by M. Vasalis, the pseudonym of one of Holland's best-known women poets of the early post-war period. Her theme bears a strong resemblance to that of Frederik van Eeden's poem which you heard at the beginning, but her treatment of it is very different.

HE CRIES...

He cries, and from his eyes that sleep has turned
to stone, the tears leap out,
like water struck from rock;

they hang like lanterns from each lash,
they sparkle on his pallid cheek,
his tiny face is firm and proud:
he cries, and yet he seems unmoved.

He is alone, held upright in my arm,
alone in his midget world, I cannot warm
him, comfort him, when in sleep
his body shudders, tangled in his dream.

Until he wakes and listens to my voice,
stares at my face, and as I sing to him,
suddenly knows me, smiles through tear-glazed eyes,
and opens all his doors and lets me in.

Hij huilt...
(Translated by James Brockway)

YOUTH

Although the heading here is Youth, this time we shall not be presenting literature *about* youth, but literature *by* youth, by a few of the many younger writers who have begun their careers since the war.

On July 26, 1950, a young Dutch poet died, at the age of 26. His name was Hans Lodeizen. At the time of his death he had published only one small collection, but his poetry had made so deep an impression that two years later a 188-page volume of his poems was published, selected by three of Holland's leading poets—a striking yet fitting tribute to a true poet. Lodeizen's voice is a melancholy, yet far from depressing voice: one which in sensuous verses, with a form and mood all their own, expressed a longing for a world subtler and kinder than the world as he found it. It was a voice, to quote the English title he gave to one of his poems, 'wise yet stammering'. Here is a translation of that poem:

> *people of course will say again:*
> *no you don't speak for us*
> *your voice is an internal thunderstorm;*
> *not in my line, you can count me out*
> *people will turn their backs on me*
>
> *and they're right of course they're right*
> *but a thunderstorm no soft music*
> *on a spinet issuing from a little summerhouse,*
> *hanging on cobwebs*
> *on a Sunday morning, with a princess.*
>
> *how far the calendar is*
> *from my hands how high*
> *time hangs above my head I laugh*
> *out of sheer bewilderment I weep*
> *out of pure chagrin I live,*
> *they say I am a living being*
> *Mine the responsibility*

I might die they say
and then, they say . . .

And in the following brief poem, Lodeizen seems to be promising himself and his friends a great happiness he knew could never be his:

I shall come back to you
and the year will be a feast,
the people will embrace me
the wind will greet me
and I shall float on your hands
like a ship

I've been away for long enough,
I toy with the wistful thread of time,
cry, laugh, talk a bit, cry, laugh,
and acquaint myself with the flexibility of grief.
I shall come back to you like a ship.

(Translations by James Brockway)

Hans Lodeizen's success seemed to open the way to the Experimentalists, the young Dutch poets of the 'fifties, who, as he did, cast off the old, traditional forms of poetry and began to write a poetry of their own, full of surrealist and dadaist effects, a poetry often reminiscent of the paintings of Marc Chagall.

One of the leading Experimentalists is a poet known by the pseudonym of Lucebert, a colourful and original conjurer with words. He was born in 1924. Here is a poem typical of his early manner:

I'm reeling off a little revolution,
I'm reeling off a lovely, little revolution,
I'm no longer of land,
I'm of water again.

I bear foaming whitehorses on my head,
I bear shooting phantoms in my head,

On my back a mermaid rests,
On my back rests the wind.
The wind and the mermaid sing,
The foaming whitehorses hiss,
The shooting phantoms fall.

I'm reeling off a lovely, little, rustling revolution,
And I fall and I hiss and I sing.

(Translated by James Brockway)

Another is Remco Campert, born in 1929. Though resembling Lodeizen's in some ways, Campert's poetry has a colder, bitterer quality about it and is less sensuous, as the following poem may show:

COLD

Winter approaches.
I can feel it in the light
and in the words I use.
Everything is becoming clearer; you can see
to the very end of the street. Words
have no end.

I am nearer
to the truth in December
than in July. I am a poet,
it seems, by the grace of the calendar.
But it's the towns, not words,
which are approaching their end.

If only somewhere,
summer and winter, a star shone,
shedding a fierce, white light.
I say a star, yet it could be
anything. As long as it burns
and gives warmth to words.

But I don't believe in
such a star, still less
in wintertime. In words
I have to believe. Yet who
can do that? I am a voice,
cold and dying,
full of wintry words.

(Translated by James Brockway)

The work of nearly all the younger writers represents a protest, a protest against their environment, in which they feel ill at ease. Many have found a refuge from this in love, in a private relationship with a single individual, and their poetry then often gains in warmth and coherence. Here, in the following short poem by Remco Campert, this is very obvious—his voice no longer being 'full of wintry words'.

LIFE WITH YOU

Aglow from head to toe
as though I'm being scourged
and caressed
by a sun and a storm.

How you fill me, sweet rain,
through my two ears,
till I'm a gourd,
bursting with love.

Like stories that thrilled me
when I was a boy,
you set all my world
atremble:

the forest's on fire
and we open our homes
to each other's flames.

(Translated by James Brockway)

The same can be found in recent poetry by Hans Andreus, born in 1926 and one of the most individual figures among the younger Dutch poets. Yet in this poem a note of bitterness is retained:

FOR A TOMORROW

If I die tomorrow
tell it to the trees,
how much I loved you.
Tell it to the wind
that clambers in the trees
or out of the branches falls,
how much I loved you.
Tell it to a child
that's young enough to understand,
tell it to some beast, perhaps
merely by gazing in its eyes,
tell it to the houses of bricks and stone,
tell it to the town,
how much I loved you.

But tell it not to men,
They would never believe you,
they would simply hate to believe
that mere man could love mere woman,
as I loved you.   (Translated by James Brockway)

The same influences have been at work among the younger generation of writers in Belgium. Here the dominating figure is Hugo Claus, born in 1929. An enormously energetic writer, Claus has not only published volumes of poetry, novels and short stories, but is a well known and highly successful playwright, two of his most telling plays being 'A Bride in the Morning' and 'Sugar'. His work has been translated into several languages. He is also the translator of Dylan Thomas's famous radio play 'Under Milk Wood'.

Another young Flemish poet and author is Jos Vandeloo who has won great success with his short novel 'Danger' based on the problems of the

Atomic Age. Here is a translation of one of his prose poems.

SPLINTERS HAVE SHARP EDGES

There was a man who always walked along the street
looking for something. No one knew what. He would keep
his eyes fixed on the cobbles. You scarcely ever saw
his face. It was always turned to the ground.

In former times, on the contrary, he had always looked upwards.
He would walk with his head bent over backwards, his eyes
sweeping the sky like searchlights, as though he was hoping to
discover something, to catch something. He was an idiot,
people said.

He was simply a poet, looking for words.
New words to pack his feelings in,
New words to have a bathe in.

Since he found nothing, he began to walk bent over forwards
and staring at the ground. What precisely he was looking for
I don't know, for there are so many people who walk about
with their eyes fixed on the ground. Anything worth having
is soon picked up.

He went on searching like this for years, until one day
he stood still with astonishment. It's immaterial what day
it was, if it was summer or winter, morning,
afternoon, or evening. It was a busy street,
no one seemed to notice it. A sparkling it was, that
flashed up into his eyes.

It must be very valuable, he thought. It surprised him
that no one should have picked it up, that glistening
little splinter. It was very small, but it shone with
an unusually brilliant lustre. It might be platinum or
even something worth far more. He looked about him

*cautiously, bent down quickly, and snatched the gleaming
splinter up.*

*It was a strange splinter. Adazzle with light,
transparent, polished into many facets, luminous with
an inner glow. It lay in his hand and it moved as it shone
and shot brilliantly coloured sparks of light
up into his face. What could it be?
he wondered. It must be valuable. Perhaps I can sell it
and then I'll be rich.*

*But suddenly he knew what it was. It came to him in a flash,
brusquely, like a poem. He laughed when he realized what it was.
He hadn't thought of that, he said. It was the first time
in his life he had laughed. It hurt a little, it was a strange
uncomfortable movement for his muscles to have to make.*

*No one had seen it lying there. For days everybody
had been treading on it. Cautiously, he moved a little to
one side of the crowd. He would hide it away, this splinter,
Happiness (for that is what it was). It is rarer
than radium, he thought. You'll probably be able to
cure cancer with it.*

*At first he did not know where he ought to hide away his
priceless find. Then, resolute, he tucked it away
in his heart. When he knew it was safely stowed away there
he suddenly noticed his hand was bleeding, The sharp
edges of the splinter had injured his fingers.
The blood was a thin snake running across his hand.
The passers-by in the street halted
in their tracks. One of them even had pity on him.*

*He was gripped by a terrible anxiety. The splinter would
now wound his heart as well and kill him. He could already
feel the stinging pain. In his mouth he became aware of the*

D Je vlant die altijt zijn strickẽ eñ netten spreit
Haeckẽde nae die verdoemenis der sielẽ des
woorden hoorẽde seyde tot hẽ seluen aldus
Dat woert werdt mi die siele weerdich
Ick hebbe mi seluen toeghemaect rechtueerdich
Il waer ick een mensche eñ al bi gods ghedoogh
Tes al te passe sonder mijn een oghe
Die is of si mi wt waer ghesworen

Woodcut from "Mariken van Nieumeghen", post-incunabulum, Antwerp ca. 1518

*cruel taste of blood. Some one fetched him a chair to sit on,
and far, far off, he was still just able to hear someone say:
he's dead.*

(Translated by James Brockway)

The note of protest we find in the work of the postwar poets has been
even more pronounced in some recent Dutch novels. In 1947, Simon van
het Reve won the young writers' prize with a first novel entitled 'The
Evenings'. Plotless, this novel recounts the thoughts of a young man living
with his parents and highly dissatisfied with himself and his surroundings.
Though strongly criticized by some for its mocking and even sadistic attack
on the petty bourgeois environment, the novel nevertheless voiced the
mood of many of the younger generation and forms a landmark in postwar
writing. The author, now writing under his true name, Gerard Kornelis
van het Reve, has also written a brilliant story recounting the decline of a
Jewish family during the Nazi Occupation.

In the novels of W. F. Hermans, the most powerful and controversial of
novelist critics of modern Dutch society, we see a vigorous mind delivering
an even sharper and more sustained attack. Hermans' pessimistic view of
humanity is expressed in a despairing cry uttered by one character in his
latest and most compelling novel, 'The Darkroom of Damocles'. He cries
out: 'Oughtn't it to be possible to imagine a world in which people at
least don't kill each other deliberately? Surely mankind should be able to
achieve that bare minimum?'

But not all young Dutch novelists write in this vein. Harry Mulisch,
one of the most gifted, often resorts to fantasy to make his criticism, and
though he can achieve a nightmarish effect in this way, his fantasy is not
without a comic, absurd element. Another, Willem G. van Maanen, also
resorts to fantasy, but it is gentler and more whimsical, and though sometimes touching on the tragic, it is imbued with a tender humour.

In his first novel, 'Life's a Dream', Van Maanen retells in a modern
setting the medieval Dutch legend of Mary of Nymegen, a girl who is
seduced by the devil in human guise but rescued by the Virgin Mary.
Among the characters in the book is an impoverished student of philosphy,
Vosmaer, and in the following passage, we find him lying in his garret,

making nonsensical speeches to an imaginary audience about the various objects in his room. He finally lights upon the water jug.

'For some time now the water jug has been occupying his attention, and he feels an urge to make it quite clear to himself (and his audience) precisely why this is. It's an old-fashioned, white, earthenware jug, with a garland of red flowers painted round the base and the brim. On the one side the potter has pinched a spout, on the other he has attached an elegant ear. It's that ear, says the student, that ear which intrigues me. It seems to be listening, and not simply because it's a metaphor either. It's alive and it imbues the whole jug with life. It gives it its shape. The position of the ear determines that of the spout. If I regard the spout as a nose, it is clear that it is located where the second ear is to be found in man. This identification of ear with spout, he continues, should cause us no surprise. We need only think of the saying, 'When the liquor's in the man, Wisdom's in the can'—where, of course, the word 'can' means 'jug'.

Now Vosmaer has really got into his stride. He is swept along in the forward surge of his thoughts. He feels he has begun to comprehend something of the Incomprehensible. He turns round on to his side, so that he can still keep an eye on the jug and at the same time face his audience squarely. Man is to can as ear is to spout! he announces. One could also say: What the ear is to the man, the spout is to the can—though, that, I suspect, is devoid of meaning. Such an expression does, nevertheless, demonstrate what a can, i.e. a jug, means to man. Otherwise he would never look upon a can as the repository of wisdom. That single ear on my water jug receives words and sounds and transmits them to the jug. The jug transforms them into wisdom, which the spout, in its turn, pours out!

Oh, Language! Vosmaer cries out, rising from his semi-recumbent posture, exponent of all hidden wisdom, consummator of our every unconscious thought, silent guide down the winding pathways of the human mind! And he decides there and then to include the can, i.e. the jug, in his dissertation, after first having published an article on it in a journal of philosophy.'

(Translated by James Brockway)

INDEX

Page.

Aafjes, Bertus (born 1914)   24
  *Amorous Ditty in the Early Morn**   24
Achterberg, Gerrit (1905-1962)   41
  *Divining Rod**   41
Alphen, Hieronymus van (1746-1803)   80
Andreus, Hans (born 1926)   91
  *For a Tomorrow**   91
Anonymous Poets (mediaeval)   14, 27, 44, 74, 95
  Ballads   20
  Floris ende Blanchefloer   27
  Lanseloet   27
  *Egidius, where are you hiding**   37, 38
  *The Song of the Churls**   67
  Mary of Nijmegen   95
Anonymous Poet (± 1570)   43
  *Wilhelmus**   12, 43
Beets, Nicolaas (1814-1903)   12, 27
  Camera Obscura   12, 27
Bilderdijk, Willem (1756-1831)   32, 44
  *Prayer**   32
Blaman, Anna (1905-1960)   41
  *A Matter of Life and Death**   42
Bloem, J. C. (born 1887)   18, 50, 52
  *After the Liberation**   19
  *Dapper Street**   50, 51
Bordewijk, F. (born 1884)   51, 52
  *Blossoming Branch**   51, 52
Boutens, P. C. (1870-1943)   46
  *Heart and Country**   46
Bredero, G. A. (1585-1618)   12, 25
  *A Peasant's Party**   25
Busken Huet, G. (1826-1886)   25, 56, 58
  *The Land of Rembrandt**   56
Campert, Jan (1902-1943)   77
  *The Song of the Eighteen Dead**   77
Campert, Remco (born 1929)   89, 80
  *Cold**   89
  *Life with You**   90
Carmiggelt, Simon (born 1913)   28
  *Lantern Slides**   28
Claus, Hugo (born 1929)   91
  A Bride in the Morning   91
  Sugar   91

	Page.
Couperus, Louis (1863-1923)	16, 82
Essays*	16
Short Stories*	82
Dante	9
Decker, Jeremias de (1609-1666)	15
Now the Heavens open wide	15
Deken, Aagje (1741-1904)	12, 80
Sara Burgerhart	80
Deijssel, Lodewijk van (1864-1952)	22
A Love Affair*	22
Donne, John	12
Douwes Dekker, Eduard,	
see Multatuli	
Dylan Thomas	91
Eeden, Frederik van (1860-1932)	80
Little Johan	80
His First Smile*	80
Eyck, P. N. van (1887-1954)	39
Oh, Death, Mysterious Nightingale	39
The Gardener and Death*	40
Engelman, Jan (born 1900)	58
Titus Reading	58
Erasmus	9, 10
The Praise of Folly	9, 10
Experimentalists	88
Frank, Anne (1929-1945)	48
Diary	48, 77
Genestet, P. A. de (1829-1861)	45
Such is Holland*	45
Gezelle, Guido (1830-1899)	33
Prayer*	33
Gorter, Herman (1864-1927)	15
May*	16
Heine, Heinrich	27
Helmers, J. F. (1767-1813)	44
The Dutch Nation	44
Hermans, W. F. (born 1921)	95
The Darkroom of Damocles	95
Heyermans, Herman (1864-1924)	63
The Good Hope	63
Hofmannsthal, Hugo von	37
Hooft, Pieter Corneliszoon (1581-1647)	12, 20, 49
Love Sonnet*	20
Hoornik, Eduard (born 1910)	53, 85
My Daughter and I*	85
Amsterdam*	53
Horace	68

Page.

Huygens, Constantijn (1596-1687)   12, 50, 52
   Towns with Voices   50
   Amsterdam Speaks*   50
Keats   15
Kloos, Willem (1859-1938)   62
   The Sea*   62
Legends (mediaeval)   31
   Beatrice   11, 31
Lodeizen, Hans (1924-1950)   87
   'Voice wise yet stammering ...'*   87
   I shall come back to you*   89
Looy, Jacobus van (1855-1930)   82
Lucebert (born 1924)   88
   I'm reeling of a little revolution*   88
Maanen, Willem G. van (born 1920)   95
   Life's a Dream*   95, 96
Marsman, H. (1899-1940)   41, 47, 61
   Porta Nigra   41
   Thinking of Holland*   47
Milton
Minne, Richard (born 1891)   18
   Beautiful Day*   18
Mulisch, Harry (born 1927)   95
Multatuli (Eduard Douwes Dekker,   12, 74, 80
1820-1887)
   Woutertje Pieterse   80
   Max Havelaar   12, 74
   Thugatèr*   75
Nijhoff, Martinus (1894-1953)   36
   The Soldier Who Crucified Christ*   36
Paaltjens, Pieter (1835-1894)   27
   Sobs and Grins   27
Perron, Edgar du (1899-1940)   41, 84
   The Child We Were*   84
   Prayer to Obdurate Death   41
Petrus van Diest (± 1500)   37
   Everyman (Elckerlijc)   11, 37
Plato   47
Poot, Hubert Corneliszoon   47
(1689-1733)   68, 80
   The Farmer's Life*   69
Potgieter, E. J. (1808-1875)   44
   Holland*   44
   Reinaert de Vos   11
Reve, Simon van het (born 1923)   95
   The Evenings   95
Roland Holst, A. (born 1888)   62

	Page.
Roland Holst, Henriëtte (1869-1952)	77
Sacred Songs and Carols (mediaeval)	31
The Three Kings*	31
Schendel, Arthur van (1874-1946)	22
Moonlight*	22
Shakespeare	9, 25
Shelley	15
Slauerhoff, J. (1898-1936)	64
Life on Eearth	65
Spinoza	47
Staring, A. C. W. (1767-1840)	21
Recollection*	21
Streuvels, Stijn (born 1871)	70
De Vlaschaard*	70
Stuiveling, Garmt (born 1907)	59
Saskia*	59
Tachtigers (Men of the eighties)	15, 62
Thomas a Kempis	9
Imitation of Christ	9
Valerius, Adriaen (± 1575-1625)	74
O, Nederland let op Uw Saeck*	74
Vandeloo, Jos (born 1925)	91
Danger	91
Splinters have Sharp Edges*	92
Vasalis, M. (born 1909)	86
He cries*	86
Vestdijk, Simon (born 1898)	55, 63
Self-portrait*	55
The Brown Friend*	63
Vondel, Joost van den (1587-1679)	12, 32, 38, 46, 49, 52, 61, 80
My Daughter Departing...*	38, 80
Adam in Exile	32
Hymn to the Godhead	32
Lucifer	12, 32
On Amstelredam	49
Walschap, Gerard (born 1898)	34
The Treatment of Christ*	34
Werumeus Buning, J. W. F.	72
(1891-1958)	
The Ballad of the Farmer*	72
Woestijne, Karel van de (1878-1929)	40
The Farmer Who Dies	41
Wolff, Betje (1738-1804)	12, 80
Sara Burgerhart	80
Yeats, W. B.	62
Zola, Emile	

8 1116